BK0003

KEYWORDS
IN THE
TEACHING OF JESUS

D1733381

KEYWORDS

IN THE

TEACHING OF JESUS

BY

A. T. ROBERTSON, D. D.

BAKER BOOK HOUSE
Grand Rapids, Michigan

Paperback edition issued 1977
by Baker Book House

ISBN: 0-8010-7645-5

PHOTOLITHOPRINTED BY CUSHING - MALLOY, INC.
ANN ARBOR, MICHIGAN, UNITED STATES OF AMERICA
1977

To

THE MEMORY OF
MY MOTHER WHO TAUGHT
ME TO LOVE JESUS

PREFACE

THE seven chapters in this little book were delivered as lectures to the Jackson Springs Summer Assembly, under the auspices of the Baptist State Convention of North Carolina, in the last week of June, 1904. They are published practically as they were delivered and at the request of the Assembly. Many delightful memories come thronging my mind as I now write, memories of the wood robins caroling in the pine trees as I tried to talk to a large and deeply spiritual and sympathetic audience about the words of Jesus. If a still larger audience can be led to earnest study of the Master's teaching, this volume will not be in vain. These seven lectures are not an exhaustive discussion of the teaching of Christ. No book is that, but this one only claims to set forth the main points in Christ's teaching around which the rest clings.

The first chapter discusses the same theme as the author's book, "The Teaching of Jesus Concerning God the Father," American Tract Society, New York, 1904. It is not, however, a copy of that book, nor a mere condensation of it, but an entirely independent treatment, though the same theological position is taken.

Mary chose to sit at the feet of Jesus and learn of him.   That is the place for every disciple of the Lord.

A. T. ROBERTSON

LOUISVILLE, KY.

TABLE OF CONTENTS

KEYWORDS IN THE TEACHING OF JESUS

CHAPTER I

GOD THE FATHER

"He that hath seen me hath seen the Father" (John 14 : 9).

JESUS is the great Teacher of all time. There had been great teachers before him, Confucius, Buddha, Zoroaster, Socrates. Each taught many high and noble ideals. Each left a strong mark on the life of men. Great teachers have come since the time of Jesus, some who show no trace of his influence, as Epictetus and Marcus Aurelius. We would detract naught from the glory of these men. But when all is said, the Teacher of teachers is Jesus. His words alone always proclaim eternal principles. Truth is axiomatic, if it is fundamental. Jesus dared to say that he was the Truth. No other man can say that and tell the truth. The significant thing is that men recognize that this claim is true. His kingdom, as he said to Pilate, is that of truth. This is his realm. This is not the main thing that Jesus came to do, to teach the truth. What he did is more than what he said. What he is, is more than either. He was not a mere teacher, however great. Let us never forget that. Preaching and practice with him were not separated. And preaching with him was teaching. He was no mere setter-forth of orthodox phrases, no mere stickler for the forms of faith, the shell of truth. In fact he was the ruthless iconoclast of his day, the foe of mere ceremonial observance. Jesus is the supreme example of the superiority of spirit over form. Hear him as he says : "It is the spirit that giveth life; the flesh profiteth nothing: the words that I have spoken unto you are spirit, and are life" (John 6 : 63). This is the chief difference between Jesus and all other teachers. The words of Jesus, then, are the Pierian spring from which men love to drink. "This is my beloved Son, in whom I am well pleased; hear ye him" (Matt. 17 : 5). Thus the Father spoke to Peter, James, and John on the mount of Transfiguration.

The first word in time and importance that we have from the new Teacher is about the Father. He was only twelve years old and had been left behind in the temple in Jerusalem. When Joseph and Mary sought him sorrowing, he said in surprise, "Knew ye not that I must be in my Father's

God is the Father

house?" (Luke 2 : 49.) Here for the first time the growing boy with dawning Messianic consciousness speaks out the throbbing secret of his heart. He *must*. The necessity is on him. And it is "my Father's house." He sustains a special relation to God the Father that is not true of other men. The first word is the key-word to his afterlife and teaching. He goes back to his Nazareth home and works obediently and humbly till his "hour" of manifestation comes. When the hour does strike and Jesus comes out of the baptismal water praying, he hears the Father say: "Thou art my beloved Son; in thee I am well pleased" (Luke 3 : 22).

The Father has formally and perhaps publicly acknowledged him as his Son. The boy of twelve had not been mistaken. The Father has called him his own Son. He will boldly claim God as his own **The Father of Jesus** Father, in a sense not true of others. True the devil challenges this claim by saying in the first temptation, "*If* thou art a Son of God" (Greek text, Matt. 4 : 3). But Jesus does not doubt. The first time he comes to Jerusalem he cries: "Make not my Father's house a house of merchandise" (John 2 : 16). On his second visit to Jerusalem during his ministry, he justifies his right to heal on the Sabbath day by calmly saying: "My Father

worketh even until now, and I work " (John 5 : 17).
The Pharisees are enraged, charging him with
making himself equal with God, but Jesus main-
tains his claim by an extended apologetic. Later
in his Galilean ministry he will even say : " All
things have been delivered unto me of my Father "
(Matt. 11 : 27). He claims also that no one
" knoweth the Father save the Son, and he to
whomsoever the Son willeth to reveal him " (*ibid.*).
" I and the Father are one " (John 10 : 30), he
asserts at the feast of Dedication. " Thou makest
thyself God," his enemies retort. Thus it goes to
the end. This word of Jesus about the Father
angers the Pharisees beyond measure. But he
dies with this high claim on his lips : " Father,
into thy hands I commend my spirit " (Luke
23 : 46).

Jesus is able to reveal the Father to whomsoever he wills (Matt. 11 : 27). Others, then, can
know the Father and be his chil-
The Father of dren ; not, however, in the same
All who Believe
in Jesus sense that Jesus is his Son. He
taught men to say : " Our Father
which art in heaven, hallowed be thy name " (Matt.
6 : 9). But not all are children of God in the
sense of actual enjoyment of spiritual blessings.
The younger son had gone into a far country.
When he came to himself he said : " I will arise

and go to my father " (Luke 15 : 18). But he knows that he is no more worthy to be called a son. He says frankly : " Father, I have sinned against heaven, and in thy sight." This confession is the hard thing to say, and this is why so many men never become Christians. But this is the only way to come back to the Father. Jesus put the divine side of the great initial spiritual change thus to Nicodemus : " Except a man be born anew, he cannot see the kingdom of God " (John 3 : 3). There is then a line of cleavage between men. Some are without, some are within the kingdom of God. But all who are within had to "enter the kingdom." Indeed, Jesus flatly told the Pharisees of Jerusalem that God was not their Father. "Ye are of your father, the devil " (John 8 : 44).

The sinner is not like the beast of the field. He was made in the image of God, and that likeness was a spiritual likeness. God is the Father of our spirits as well as of our bodies (Heb. 12 : 9). We are indeed, rebellious children. We have left the Father's home and spurned the Father's love. We are practically outcast children, but outcast not by the Father's wish. We have made it impossible for the Father to deal with us as sons. We are subjects of the just wrath of the Father. We are by nature

But in One Sense God is the Father of all Men

sinful, as Jesus implies by his insistence on the necessity of the new birth. If we knew the horrible reality of sin, we could understand how the Father cannot let the unrepentant sinner belong to his family. But there is a hope for the sinner. He still has a spiritual nature, however blurred. He is still kin to God and is open to the work of the Spirit of God, else all hope would be lost. It is not enough to be the child of Abraham by descent and actually a child of the devil. The real child of Abraham is the spiritual descendant. So the lost child must be found, the dead must come to life again.

Jesus builds his teaching on the Old Testament. He commended the Jews for reading the Scriptures,
The Old Testament View of the Father
for they " bear witness of me" (John 5 : 39). In the Old Testament God is the Father in the sense of Creator of all. He is also the Father of Israel in a special sense. He is the King of the kingdom of Israel and the Father of the family. What the Jews failed to understand was that the spiritual Israel was the real Israel, the spiritual kingdom the real kingdom of God. Thus the Gentiles as well as the Jews really became children of the Father. " Ye offspring of vipers " (Matt. 12 : 34), Jesus called the Pharisees who plumed themselves on being children of Abraham. " If

ye were children of Abraham, ye would do the works of Abraham" (John 8 : 39). So John the Baptist said : "Think not to say within yourselves, we have Abraham for our Father : for I say unto you that God is able of these stones to raise up children unto Abraham" (Matt. 3 : 9).

This is the most distinctive word that Jesus has to offer as a teacher of men. He has new light to give about God. It is the same kind of light that they already had in the Old Testament Scriptures. But their own traditions and sermons had darkened this light. Socrates was put to death by the Athenians for new doctrine about strange divinities, so they charged. Will the Jews stand new light from Jesus about God? This is precisely the trouble with the ancient Pharisees and their modern representatives. They are encased in a shell of ignorant omniscience. In fact, says Jesus : "Ye do err, not knowing the Scriptures nor the power of God" (Matt. 22 : 29). He knows "who the Father is" (Luke 10 : 22). And no one else has seen the Father (John 6 : 46). "Lord, shew us the Father, and it sufficeth us" (John 14 : 8), Philip pleaded. So it will. *That* is the acme of wisdom, to know God. Hear Jesus again : "O righteous Father, the world knew thee not, but I knew thee ; and these know that thou

The New Light from Jesus about the Father

didst send me; and I made known unto them thy name, and will make it known, that the love wherewith thou lovest me may be in them and I in them" (John 17 : 25 f.). Once more he says: "I glorified thee on the earth" (John 17 : 4).

Jesus claims to know the way. What is it? It is simple and plain: "*I* am the way" (John 14 : 6). He is the way to the Father. When Thomas was at a loss, this was the answer. He adds: "No one cometh to the Father, but by me" (John 14 : 6). He is not merely a way; he is *the only* way. Herein lies the supreme value of Christianity. It offers Jesus to men, the only way to God the Father. Here is the call for mission effort at home and abroad. Here is the incentive for evangelical work, for educational effort, for pressing Christ on the hearts of men, for said Jesus, "He that honoreth not the Son honoreth not the Father which sent him" (John 5 : 23). When Philip doubted, Jesus replied: "Have I been so long time with you, and dost thou not know me, Philip? he that hath seen me hath seen the Father" (John 14 : 9). Indeed, he asks: "How sayest thou, Shew us the Father?" Philip had seen Jesus. More than the words of Jesus about the Father is Jesus himself. He is the Son and is in the image of the Father. "I am in the Father and the Father in me" (John 14 : 11). The way to know the Father is to know Jesus, for the Father is like Jesus. "He that seeth me, seeth him that sent me" (John 12 : 45).

The Father loves the world that he has made, but most of all the men made in his own image. When the prodigal son was returning home, "while he was yet afar off, his father saw him, and was moved with compassion, and ran, and fell on his neck, and kissed him" (Luke 15 : 20). This is the picture that Jesus has drawn of the Father's compassionate yearning for his rebellious and outcast children. To the resentful elder son the Father said : "This thy brother was dead, and is alive again; and was lost, and is found" (Luke 15 : 32). Hence Jesus came to die for sinful men, not for animals, for sinful men are lost children of God.

The Father's Yearning for the Sinner

The yearning love of the Father does not relax the Father's justice. He will not out of hand forgive the sinner. There had to be adjustment, reconciliation. Here is the real grace of God the Father. "For God so loved the world, that he gave his only-begotten Son, that whosoever believeth on him should not perish, but have eternal life" (John 3 : 16). The love is on God's

The Father's Effort to Save the Sinner

part first. This great love provides the basis of reconciliation, the death of the Son on the cross. "So must the Son of Man be lifted up" (John 3 : 14). He gave "his life a ransom for many" (Matt. 20 : 28). From the very first Jesus is conscious that his death is necessary as the sacrifice for sin. To John the Baptist he is "the Lamb of God that taketh away the sin of the world" (John 1 : 29). It is not a surprise to Jesus when he comes to die. He not only knew it, but had interpreted it as the Father's plan for the redemption of men. But the atoning death of Jesus in the sinner's stead is only the basis of reconciliation. The work is not completed till the sinner is born again, repents, trusts the Father, and returns a suppliant to the throne of grace. The atoning death was an objective fact; the reconciling grace works in the inner spirit. This is the Father's plan of salvation as outlined by Jesus.

Of this the sinner may be sure. "There is joy in heaven over one sinner that repenteth" (Luke 15 : 7). "Let us eat and make A Welcome for merry: for this my son was dead, the Repentant and is alive again; and was lost, Sinner and is found" (Luke 15 : 32). Jesus is the way to the Father and he speaks for himself thus : "All that which the Father giveth me shall come unto me ; and him that cometh to

me I will in no wise cast out" (John 6 : 37).
This is true also : " No man can come unto me
except the Father which sent me draw him " (John
6 : 44).   We leave unsolved the reconciliation of
this initial drawing of the Father by the Holy
Spirit with the gracious invitation of Jesus who
said : " Come unto me all ye that labor and are
heavy laden and I will give you rest " (Matt. 11 :
28).   In the realm of spirit the mystery of the
freedom of our spirits and the sovereignty of God
is solved.   Let us exercise our freedom and trust
God to exercise his sovereignty.   He is responsible
for that, not we, and we can trust the Father to
do right even when we cannot understand his
plans.   We may be sure that his sovereign will is
not a hindrance, but a help to our weakness.

The Father is merciful and has shown it by the
highest of all proofs.   He held not back his own
Son.   Yet the inexorable law stands,
for all who do not make peace with   The Father as
the Father through Christ.   Jesus   Judge
himself will act as judge, it is true (John 5 : 22),
but he will execute the will of the Father.   Condemnation rests on the unrepentant sinner.   The
penalty of the Father's law will fall from the lips of
him who came to set us free from that law.   Jesus,
the Saviour, will say : " Depart from me, ye that
work iniquity " (Matt. 7 : 23).   " I never knew you."

Jesus does not often use theological terms. He sets vital truths in living speech, not in abstract phrase. Perhaps this is one reason why the people hung on his words.

What about the Character of the Father?

The Father is eternal. Jesus speaks of the glory which he had with the Father before the world was (John 17 : 5). The Father is personal as this same passage shows. He and the Father had blessed converse with each other before the objective universe came into existence. Jesus is not troubled by the philosophical theories of pantheism or monism. He knows that he exists ; he knows also that the Father exists. God is spirit, he tells the woman of Samaria (John 4 : 24). Hence materialism is untrue as well as pantheism. God is spirit, not body. We are like God in having a spiritual nature with which we must worship him. God does not make his abode simply in this place or that, neither in Gerizim nor Jerusalem. The Father, again, is almighty. "With God all things are possible" (Matt. 19 : 26). And the Father is good, absolutely good. "None is good save one, even God" (Luke 19 : 18). God is one. "Our God is one Lord," not many (Mark 12 : 29). He is once more "the living Father" (John 6 : 57). Thus does Jesus speak of his Father and our Father. He had been in the bosom of the Father and was able to declare the Father to men (John 1 : 18). No one else has seen the Father (John 6 : 46). Hence no one else can declare the Father.

It is not an absentee God that Jesus set forth to men. " My Father worketh even until now " (John 5 : 17). He cares for the lilies of the field, he watches the sparrows when they fall, he counts the hairs of our heads. With Jesus **The Father is Present in His World** the Father is the ever-present reality. The world is transient and unstable. The world is the seeming, the Father the real. But the Father's hand is over all.

This is mysticism to us, but not to Jesus. He was in the Father and the Father in him. He prayed that the disciples might be one in the Father and the Son (John 17 : 21). Indeed, he said : " If a man love me he will keep my word : **The Father Dwells in His Children** and my Father will love him, and we will come unto him, and make our abode with him " (John 14 : 23). That is to bring heaven down to earth, for heaven is where God is. It was to do just this thing that Jesus left the glory of heaven that he might find the key to human hearts. The happiness of Jesus consists in bringing men back to God, to make reconciliation possible, to break down the middle wall of partition between God and man, between Jew and Gentile, to establish a real brotherhood of redeemed souls. He has taught us how the Father loves us. He has shown us what the Father is like. He has taught us to say, "Our Father." In his hour of anguish he himself cried, "Abba, Father." He offers to take us by the hand and put our hand in the Father's and be our Elder Brother. "If ye had known me, ye should have known my Father also; and from henceforth ye know him, and have seen him" (John 14 : 7). For "this is life eternal, that they might know thee the only true God, and Jesus Christ whom thou hast sent" (John 17 : 3).

CHAPTER II

THE SON

"Take my yoke upon you, and learn of me, for I am meek and lowly in heart" (Matt. 11 : 29).

JESUS has to speak of himself in order to set forth the Father. He does not talk of himself just to be speaking about himself.

It would be egotistic in anybody else to speak of himself as our Lord does. Egotism is more than a weakness. It is abnormal, is a species of insanity, more or less severe. So Paul exhorted the Roman Christians so to think as to think soberly and not to think of themselves more highly than they ought to think (Rom. 12 : 3). "Let another man praise thee." This is the universal opinion of the world. Self-assertion is necessary to effective work; a cringing self-repression is pitiful, but self-conceit is repulsive. Why, then, can we retain our love and adoration for Jesus, if he spoke so much of himself? It is because he was more than man. If he was merely a man, even the greatest of men, the terms that he uses of himself would be intoler-

The Son's Egoism

able, as for instance, "I am the light of the world" (John 8 : 12). It is in the high relations that Jesus holds with the Father, in what he is, that he escapes the charge of egotism.

In his "Intimations of Immortality" Words-worth pictures the soul as dimly conscious of a

The Pre-incarnate State of Jesus

previous existence. We may well dismiss such poetic fancies. But what shall we say of the repeated statements of Jesus on this subject concerning himself ? "Before Abraham was, I am" (John 8 : 58); "I came out from the Father, and am come into the world" (John 16 : 28); "the glory which I had with thee before the world was" (John 17 : 5). We may well agree with the claim of Jesus that "a greater than Solomon is here" and "a greater than Jonah" (Luke 11 : 31 f.). It is an easy answer to say that Jesus means only ideal pre-existence by such high words. He ex-isted in the mind of the Father, it is said. Such quibbling is puerile, for Christ is speaking of per-sonal experiences and objective facts. He had glory, existed, came forth from the Father. "For thou lovedst me before the foundation of the world" (John 17 : 24). It is far more manly to say at once that Jesus did not know what he was saying. He would then be an ignorant enthusiast, it is true. If we credit his character and his words and John's account of them, we must admit this sublime fact of his pre-existence. The Synoptic account of the virgin birth of Jesus reinforces the teaching of Christ on this point. Likewise the express statement of John that in the beginning the Word was with God (John 1 : 1). We may well stand in awe of one who can truthfully assert that he was with the Father before the world was. There is mystery here surely as to the possibility of the continuity of consciousness in such a transition, but no greater than such continuity in the case of death. In reality Christ claims timeless existence, for he said: "I am" (John 8 : 58).

"Father," "my Father," "the Father" are words often on the lips of Jesus. He was ever conscious of the peculiar intimacy between him and his Father. He likewise called himself "the Son of God" and "the Son," as the Father called him "my Son." "The Father loveth the Son" (John 5 : 20); "the hour cometh, and now is, when the dead shall hear the voice of the Son of God; and they that hear shall live" (John 5 : 25); "Dost thou believe on the Son of God?" Jesus asked the blind man who had recently been healed (John 9 : 35). When asked pointedly and under oath by Caiaphas if he was "the Christ, the Son of God," he answered, "I am" (Matt. 26 :

Christ's Relation to the Father

63 f.).   It was not often, for obvious reasons, that
Jesus so clearly asserted that he was the Son of
God.   When he did so, it aroused vehement hostility (John 5, 8, and 10).   At last his saying so
brought condemnation from the Sanhedrin.   It
was not a mere vague term for the spiritual rela-
tionship of men with God.   He meant the full
content of the words.   " I and the Father are
one " (John 10 : 30).   We may not venture farther
into the high and holy fellowship that exists between the Father and the Son.   The only begotten
Son is in the bosom of the Father, John tells us
(John 1 : 18).   He is one in nature, one in thought,
one in word, one in deed with the Father.   "All
things that the Father hath are mine " (John 16 :
15).   Jesus has life in himself as the Father has
(John 5 : 26).   Hence he could say : " I am the
life " (John 11 : 25).   Jesus, as the Father, is
ultimate life.   The scientists will never find life
by the microscope, though lower forms of life con-
tinue to be discovered.   Not even radium is life.

If these claims are true, Jesus is God as John
expressly says.   " The Word was God " (John 1 : 1).
The Divinity of Jesus   This is the clear import of the term
" the Son," "the Son of God " in
the mouth of Jesus.   " I proceeded
forth and came from God " (John 8 : 42).   " I
know him ; for I am from him " (John 7 : 29).

"Before Abraham was I am" (John 8 : 58). There is no stopping-place short of real deity in the claims of Christ. When he says : "I am the light of the world" (John 8 : 12), it is sober truth or wild self-conceit. If it is self-conceit, Jesus is abnormal and not the spiritual and moral leader of the race. He falls from his high pedestal to the ground and beneath the ground. If it is truth, he is more than man. No mere man in his senses would say it of himself. Nor could it be true of any mere man. If Jesus is only man and said that, he is beneath contempt. If he is God and said it, he is above praise. There is no middle ground. "I am the resurrection, and the life" (John 11 : 25). Here again the same argument holds. "For as the Father raiseth up the dead, and quickeneth them ; even so the Son quickeneth whom he will" (John 5 : 21). "Ye are from beneath ; I am from above : ye are of this world; I am not of this world" (John 8 : 23). "All power is given me in heaven and earth" (Matt. 28 : 18). What sane man could speak these words if he were only man ? Jesus expressly healed the paralytic let down through the roof that his enemies might "know that the Son of man hath power on earth to forgive sins" (Matt. 9 : 6). The Pharisees had rightly said that God alone could forgive sins. Moreover, all other men are conscious of sin. But

Jesus never betrays the slightest consciousness of guilt of any kind. There are varieties of religious experience among men, but all agree on this point: "We have all sinned and come short of the glory of God." But not so Jesus. On the other hand he repeatedly claims perfect obedience to the will of the Father. "My meat is to do the will of him that sent me" (John 4 : 34). He came to save sinners and had no sin of his own. This is an anomaly in human experience that cannot be explained, save on the assumption of the divinity of Jesus. In the beginning of his ministry Jesus said to Nathanael: "Verily, verily, I say unto you, Ye shall see the heavens opened, and the angels of God ascending and descending upon the Son of man" (John 1 : 51). He will make the prophecy on his trial that "the Son of man shall sit on the right hand of the power of God" (Luke 22 : 69), and he will be seen "coming in the clouds of heaven" (Mark 14 : 62).

The incarnation is the first glorious fact in the life of Jesus on earth. It is a mighty fact fraught with mystery. Jesus could, of course, say nothing about the mystery of his birth. How much his mother told him or the Father revealed to him we do not know. He called Joseph father, but he early knew that God was his true Father,

Jesus' Connection with Mankind

and at the age of twelve says "My Father" when speaking of God (Luke 2 : 51). This is not the place to discuss the virgin birth since Jesus naturally did not do so. But the words of Jesus are in harmony with what Matthew and Luke do say directly, and what John implies and Paul also, though not so strongly. In calling himself Son of God and Son of Man he presents the two-fold nature. He was divine and human. The feeling of Jesus toward his mother was loving and tender. In calling her "Woman" at Cana during the wedding feast he was not harsh (John 2 : 4), for on the cross also he addressed her thus when he commended her to the care of John (John 19 : 26). He did make her understand, after he entered upon his Messianic work, that she was not to control his actions further. Henceforth the Father and the Spirit were to direct his way. But Jesus was not ashamed to call us brethren and friends. His favorite title for himself was "the Son of Man." He joyfully acknowledged his humanity, which was real and no mere phantom. The term itself is linked to the phrase "a Son of Man" in the book of Daniel. Jesus seems to have used it to express his real humanity, the representative character of his relation to men and the ideal character of the true man. Hence he submitted to baptism, though he had no sins of which to repent (Matt. 3 : 15). Hence he endured temptation and gained power and sympathy. So he grew weak and weary, and had at times not where to lay his head (Luke 9 : 58). So he went down into the valley of trial and at the very bottom cried out : "O my Father, if it be possible, let this cup pass from me : nevertheless not as I will, but as thou wilt" (Matt. 26 : 39). Out of the darkness he exclaimed : "My God, my God, why hast thou forsaken me ?" (Matt. 27 : 46.) It cost all this for Christ to be a man, but he gladly became flesh for our sakes (2 Cor. 8 : 9).

When did our Lord first become aware that he was the Messiah, the Son of God ? Some say that he knew as much even as a babe The Messianic as he ever did. Others say that he Self-Conscious- did not know that he was the Mesness of Jesus siah till the voice of the Father so greeted him at his baptism. Both views are clearly wrong, though we must be careful not to dogmatize. When twelve years old Jesus said to Joseph and Mary in the temple : "Wist ye not that I must be in my Father's house ?" (Luke 2 : 50). Here he evidently is conscious that he sustains a peculiar relation to the Father not held by others. When he first grew into that consciousness it is idle to speculate. He did grow in wisdom as he grew in stature (Luke 2 : 52). Here is an in-

soluble mystery, how the Son of God could grow
in wisdom ; but we must be content with our ignorance.   We do not even know how our spirits can
dwell in our bodies.   Doubtless the consciousness
of his own deity grew with the years. He knows
that he is the Messiah when he comes to John the
Baptist and never falters in that conviction to the
end.   Jesus was no opportunist, seeking to pander
to the whims of the populace. He had the high
moral courage to be the true Messiah at the cost
of his life rather than be the Messiah of the crowd
with continued human life and an earthly crown.
He was, likewise, not a disappointed man. He
had full in view the issues at stake and the import
of his message and the outcome.   He will say to
the woman at the well : " I that speak unto thee
am he " (John 4 : 26).   He will say to Caiaphas
at last under oath : " I am he " (Mark 14 : 62).

He loved to speak of himself as sent by the
Father into the world (John 6 : 38 f., 57 ; 12 : 49).
He was anointed for his mission,
and hence was the Messiah, the   Jesus'
Anointed One. He did not con-   Conception of
sider himself an accident, an adven- His Mission
turer, a piece of driftwood in the centuries, or
even the result of a natural evolutionary process.
He was come to bear witness to the truth in a
world of lies (John 18 : 37).   He was come as the

light of the world in the midst of darkness (John
8 : 12; 12 : 46). He was come as the good shepherd to care for the sheep and to keep off the
wolves and the hirelings (John 10 : 1–18). He
was a physician in the midst of the sick (Matt.
9 : 12). He came to save the lost in a world of
sin (Luke 19 : 10). He came to give life in the
midst of death (John 4 : 13 f.; 6 : 55–58). He was
indeed the water of life and the bread from heaven.
In a word, he came "to preach the gospel to the
poor; he hath sent me to heal the brokenhearted,
to preach deliverance to the captives, and recover-
ing of sight to the blind, to set at liberty them
that are bruised, to preach the acceptable year
of the Lord" (Luke 4 : 18). He was ready to
do this if it cost his life, as he knew it would.
He came "to give his life a ransom for many"
(Matt. 20 : 28).

It was the Father's love for the world that
caused him to send the Son into the world (John
3 : 16). At every turn Jesus mani-
Christ's Love fested his own pity and love for a
for ruined race. He was known as the
the World friend of publicans and sinners and
defended his search for the worst sinners. He
had the shepherd heart that would go out after
the lost lamb on the mountain. He offered the
water of life to all who would come and drink

(John 7 : 37), rest to all the weary and the sin-sick and the heavy laden (Matt. 11 : 28 f.).

He linked his teaching to that of the Old Testament, and distinctly denied that he came to destroy the law and the prophets, but rather to fulfil. To fulfil is to make full. He came to complete, to realize, to go farther in the same direction. *Jesus' Teaching and the Old Testament* Where the Old Testament was symbolical, he was the reality. Where the Old Testament was ceremonial, he was spiritual and ethical. Where the Old Testament was type and shadow, he gave the substance. Where the Old Testament was negative, Christ was positive. Where the Old Testament was a concession to the weakness of human nature, Jesus struck off the outer shell and went to the heart of the matter. But Jesus ever exalted the Old Testament, even when he said, "I say unto you," in contrast with its commands. It was not a contrast in kind, but in degree. He caught the spirit of the Old Testament and released men from the bondage of the letter. So the Sermon on the Mount does not decry the Old Testament, but exalts it. "Hate thine enemy" (Matt. 5 : 43) is not in the Old Testament, but is the teaching of the rabbis. Jesus brought life and immortality to light, "the light of the gospel of the glory of Christ."

But Jesus does set himself against the teachers of the time, who had covered up the spirit of the Old Testament with their traditions and legends and hair-splitting theories. The theology of Jesus runs counter to the theology of his day at a number of essential points. He had to expose the hypocrisy of the Pharisees, their mere formalism, their literalism as to the Sabbath, their burdensome rules about everyday life, their worldly-mindedness, their error as to a temporal kingdom, their spiritual blindness. In a word: "Except your righteousness exceed the righteousness of the scribes and Pharisees, ye shall in no wise enter the kingdom of heaven" (Matt. 5 : 20). This necessary antagonism of Jesus lashed the Pharisees into a fury and they early began to plot for his death. They could not brook such teaching. He was a heretic and must be exterminated.

The Current Teaching

Jesus did not falter. He rose above the false clamor of approval from the people and the din of opposition from the Jerusalem conspiracy. He knew that he was the Son of God and had a message for men. He brushed aside the cobwebs of tradition and rabbinical technicalities and gave men the truth. It was the very breath of heaven, and men marveled at his words. He spoke

The Sense of Authority in Jesus

not as the scribes, but with authority. It was a
new day in Palestine when the truth could be
turned loose on its own merits without the support
of some great name to guarantee its genuineness.
The modern era began with Jesus in more senses
than one. The Dark Ages in after years was an
effort to hold down the light. His kingdom was
truth and he could stand and look down on Pilate's
timid cowardice. Jesus dared call men to himself.
"I am the truth" (John 14 : 6), he said. We think
of truth as a system. Jesus incarnated it and we
can grasp truth in its fulness only as we get close
to him. This is the fault with one-sided scientists
and narrow theologians. He invited men to come
and take his yoke, come to school to him, for his
yoke is easy and his burden is light. The lessons
are not hard after we get a start. And we can sit
like Mary at the Teacher's feet and learn of him.
This is not conceit in Jesus, but the natural unfolding of what he was to those who needed him.

He had much to give as a Teacher. The Father
revealed to him the wisdom of heaven. He was
under the guidance of the Holy
Spirit. He was the Son of God. The Knowledge
of Jesus
Peter finally was able to say to him :
"Lord, thou knowest all things" (John 21 : 17), and
it was true. And yet he grew in knowledge, was
surprised at various times, and on one occasion

said that he knew not when the day of the end of the world would be (Mark 13 : 32). Here we confront a mystery past our unraveling. It is one thing not to know and another to know wrongly. If Jesus had human limitations in his knowledge on certain points, and so did not speak on them, we may not call him in error when he does speak. Least of all may we say that Jesus was ignorant of the Old Testament, for here he expressly claimed to have new light and chided the teachers of his time with their ignorance and error. Nor must we let our own ignorance on this subject accent unduly the supposed ignorance of Jesus.

The central teaching of Jesus was his death and resurrection. If we wish to learn the theology of Jesus, we must follow his lead. He is his own best interpreter. He laid accent on his miracles and urged that they corroborated his claims. But they were only means to an end. He asserted that he was the Son of God and had come to save men by his death if they believed in him. He would give proof of his Messianic claims and of the power of his atoning death by rising from the dead. He had power to lay down his life and he had power to take it again. He would give his life for the sheep. He would give his life a ransom for many. His blood would be shed for the remission of sins (Matt.

26 : 28). And if he was lifted up, he would draw all men unto him (John 12 : 32). It was a voluntary death and a conscious sacrifice. He knew what he was doing and went to the cross with high and holy purpose. If he faltered for a moment in Gethsemane, that was due to the weakness of the flesh, and it was only for a moment. We must put the accent where Jesus does. He was born at all only to die for our sins. Else he had no message to teach that was other than ethical and ineffective. Else he could not be our King. Else he could not be our Saviour. Else he could not be our Priest. Else he could not be our Advocate. But for his atoning death, he would have been only another of the many teachers of the world. The blood of Christ makes possible the work of the Spirit. But his death on the cross and his resurrection from the grave were long in his heart and on his lips. It all fell on dull ears. But thanks be to God for the victory in a crucified and risen Saviour. Jesus had no mere mechanical conception of his atoning death. He clearly taught that he gave his life a ransom in place of those who were saved from sin (Matt. 20 : 28). But that he perceived the vital and moral aspects of this sacrifice is plain from John 12 : 24 f. His course was in harmony with nature.

The cross is now to us in some manner what it

was to Jesus, our glory and our crown. Life is linked
with death. By his death he won the right to save
us from sin. Shall we gain life in Christ? He can
give us life abundantly if we are willing to live. The
hardest word that Jesus had for his generation was :
" Ye will not come unto me that ye might have life "
(John 5 : 40). Jesus is lord of life and conqueror of
death. When the Galilean multitudes turned away
from Jesus after they learned that he was merely
a spiritual Messiah, he turned to the disciples :
" Will ye also go away? " It was Peter who said :
" Lord, to whom shall we go? Thou hast the
words of eternal life. And we have believed and
know that thou art the Holy One of God" (John
6 : 68 f.). Peter indeed seems to have considered
going with the multitude who had left Christ, but
on the whole he had decided to hold fast to him.
His loyalty was the result of reflection, and not
mere impulse.

CHAPTER III

" To give his life a ransom for many " (Matt. 20 : 28).

THERE is not much said by Jesus about sin on
its theological side, though he has much to say
about special acts of sin.   Jesus was practical
in his teaching about the sins of men.   But the
dark shadow of sin`rested over his earthly life.   It
was in the air about him, in the lives of men and
women all around him, in the hearts of all whom
he met.   It was repulsive to his holy nature, and
yet he did not shrink from close contact with sinful
men.   Satan sought to besmirch Jesus with sin at
the start of his public work and never gave up the
hope of doing so, but tried every convenient opportunity.   He attacked Christ by every approach
possible.   In fact Christ sought out the most sinful
classes in order to help them, and was not ashamed
to be known as the friend of publicans and sinners
(Matt. 11 : 19).   But if he had sinned himself, he
could not have saved others.   His enemies jeered
at him as he hung on the cross : " He saved others ;
himself he cannot save."   That was literally true.

41

There was no doubt in the mind of Jesus about the fact of sin.   He was no dilettante re-former who had come with some rose-water nostrum to cover up the heinousness of sin.   Men have ex-hausted their ingenuity to escape the fact or the consequences of sin.   Some deny that sin is, as does the Christian Scientist.   Or it is said that sin is not so very bad after all and we can manage it without the help of Christ.   This is like the con-sumptive that is always going to get well without doing anything.   Or we are all saved by the mere fact that Christ has become man.   His incarna-tion saves the race.   A comfortable dream is this, possible only by disregarding the facts of life and the words of Jesus whose life is leaned on for salvation.

The Reality of Sin

A weakened sense of sin is the curse of our time.   Jesus had the same conception of his mis-sion that was expressed by John the Baptist, when he cried: " Behold the Lamb of God that taketh away the sin of the world " (John 1 : 29). It is the Lamb as a *sacrifice* that takes away sin. His name, Jesus, was given to him because he will save his people from their sins (Matt. 1 : 21).   He came to save sinners, not the so-called righteous (Matt. 9 : 13).   They were sinners too, but were too proud to own it, like some people now.   Let it

go at their own estimate of themselves for the
present. Here *are* sinners, who *know* that they
are sinners, and these Christ came to save, the lost
sheep. He will not have to lose time in convin-
cing these that they are sinners and lost. No
wonder the publicans and sinners came to hear
him (Luke 15 : 1). We have the same situation
to-day. The self-righteous hypocrites took the
indictment of Christ as an insult, but the publicans
knew that they were sinners. The hard field to-
day is among the self-satisfied. The coming of
Jesus quickened the consciousness of men as to sin.
" If I had not come, they had not had sin " (John
15 : 22), *i. e.*, not so great sin as they do have. And
yet Jesus had no consciousness of sin himself. In
fact, he challenged his enemies to find sin in him:
" Which of you convinceth me of sin ? " (John 8 :
46). Every sane man is conscious of sin, and is a
hypocrite if he denies it. Therefore Jesus was
God and not mere man. The Holy Spirit will
convict the world of sin (John 16 : 8), and the
preacher is helpless to move men till this personal
conviction of sin takes place. The crying need of
our day is a sharper accent on the reality of sin
and the pressure of sin on the human soul. One's
theory of God and sin decides his theology and his
life. Tell me your view of God and sin and I can
fill out the rest. The Pharisee stood and prayed

with himself (not with God) and gave the Lord
some information about his own goodness and
superiority over others.   The poor convicted publican with bowed head asked : "God be merciful
to me the sinner" (Luke 18 : 13).

As might be expected, Jesus deals with sin as a
universal fact and does not seek to explain its
origin.   He says nothing about
The Origin of   Adam and Eve and the first sin that
    Sin   entered into human hearts.   He
does not discuss the federal or the natural head-
ship of Adam.   But he treats all men as sinners
and as responsible for their sin.   "If ye were
blind, ye should have no sin" (John 9 : 41).   But
we all have conscience, a sense of right and moral
responsibility.   "Whosoever committeth sin is the
servant of sin" (John 8 : 34).   Thus he implied
that the Jews were slaves of sin and offered to
make them free indeed (John 8 : 36).   Yea, he
said : "If ye believe not that I am he, ye shall
die in your sins" (John 8 : 24).   How God could
permit sin to exist, Jesus does not say.   He has
left that for modern theologians and philosophers.
He has come to set us free from the bondage of
sin and that is better.

The modern theory of evolution is not neces-
sarily out of harmony with the essential fact of
the fall of man, the inherited sin of the race,

which lies beyond the coming of Christ to save
a lost and ruined world. Jesus calls Satan the
father of lies (John 8 : 44), and he is by implica-
tion the father of all sin. The reality and personality of Satan as the king of the kingdom of
evil, Jesus clearly teaches. No exegetical methods
can make the devil a mere personification of the
evil principle set forth in the teaching of Christ.
Satan desired to sift Simon as he had tried Jesus
and Judas. The same thing is true as to demons,
the agents of Satan. The words of Jesus are so
numerous and so explicit that the existence of demons is bound to be admitted. The possession of
men by demons is not mere disease, but the violent
exhibition of Satanic power in an effort to dominate
men. Demons may possess men now for aught
we know. The devil can change with the fashions.

Jesus makes no formal discussion of sin, but we
can get his idea of the character of sin from a
variety of arguments. He looks
upon it not as a mere disease or in-   The Nature of
firmity. The quality of sin in the   Sin
mind of Jesus is seen when he says to the Pharisees : " O generation of vipers ! how can ye, being
evil, speak good things ? " (Matt. 12 : 34.) Aliena-
tion from the Father is the worst effect of sin.
There is a break between God and men, and sin
has caused it. This is the work of Jesus, to heal

that breach.   But he does it not by patching up
sin, rather by overcoming it.   Sin makes men
blind so that "seeing they may see, and not
perceive" (Mark 4 : 12).   The deadening power
of sin affects the whole man.   This is what total
depravity means, not that there is no good in man.
But all his faculties are tainted by sin, as memory,
imagination, appetite, ambition.   The heart is
hardened ; some hearts are like the wayside, some
like the stony ground, and some like the thorny
ground.   Men are dull of hearing, with closed eyes,
with heart waxed gross, and they do not understand the mysteries of the kingdom.   Such a heart
cannot believe.   Once the Master cried out : "O
faithless and perverse generation, how long shall I
be with you ?" (Luke 9 : 41.)   The unbelief of
such hardened hearts taxed the patience of the
gentle Christ.   In some cases Jesus actually marveled at the unbelief which he met.   This is the
normal state of the human heart as the result of
sin.   Distrust of God has taken the place of love
and confidence.

Sin has its seat in the heart where are the issues
of life.   The moral life with Jesus consists in the
heart life, not in the mere outward observance.
The keenest denunciation that the Master used
was directed against the hypocrites who used the
livery of heaven to serve the devil in.   These men

outwardly appear righteous unto men, but inwardly
are full of hypocrisy and iniquity, like whited
sepulchres full of dead men's bones. The note of
genuineness is struck by Jesus with great power
and this insistence aroused the keenest hostility of
the Pharisees. God wanted heart service, not
mere lip service. It is what comes from within
that defiles the man. "Wherefore think ye evil
in your hearts?" (Matt. 9 : 4.) "The light of the
body is the eye," and "if thine eye be evil thy
whole body shall be full of darkness" (Matt.
6 : 22 f.).

Dr. James Stalker, in his recent Gay Lectures
at Louisville, pungently divided Christ's denunciation of sin into the sin of the publican, the sin of
the Sadducee, the sin of the Pharisee. The publican was guilty of sensual sin, the Sadducee of
pride, the Pharisee of hypocrisy. Jesus did not
condone the first, but found him easier to reach
than the proud Sadducee. The hypocritical Pharisee he unmercifully condemned.

With a nature thus deranged it is not strange
that men are subject to all sorts of temptations.
Jesus knew the power of temptation in his own
life and understood full well the weakness of men.
He urged the disciples to pray, "Lead us not into
temptation" (Matt. 6 : 13). In Gethsemane he
felt the full force of the tempter's power and he

besought the disciples : '" Pray that ye enter not
into temptation" (Luke 22 : 40). But he was
insistent that we resist the tempter to the end.

Besides unbelief and hypocrisy our Lord denounced other prominent sins in the people of his
time.   The pride of the rabbis, who loved to be
called "rabbi" and to have prominent seats, ex-
cited his indignation.   He told many parables to
illustrate the power of covetousness over the hearts
of those who laid up treasure for themselves and
yet were not rich toward God ; who thought that
life consisted in the abundance of the things that
one possessed.   Jesus bluntly called such men
"fools."   They missed the point of life.

Captious criticism likewise called forth the reproof of Christ.   He called attention to the fact
that the critic invited criticism on himself by
assuming such a rôle.   People in glass houses
should not throw stones, and those with beams in
their eyes had better not hunt for motes in other
people's eyes.   It was a materialistic and worldly
age to which Jesus spoke, one that loved the mammon of unrighteousness and wished to have credit
with God also.   Anger, murder, adultery, deceit,
theft, and many other sins were scathingly attacked by Christ.   Like John the Baptist he
exposed the sins of the men of the time and held
each man up before the mirror of the truth.

They did not believe on him because he told them
the truth.   Flattery and fawning tickle the fancy,
but are unthinkable in connection with Jesus.

But we do not get Christ's idea of sin till we
go with him into Gethsemane and hear him cry,
"O my Father, if it be possible, let this cup pass
away from me" (Matt. 26 : 39).   Then we know
how sinful he thought sin was.   He shrank from
the cup that he had to drink if men were to be
saved.   Go and stand by the cross and hear him
say at the conclusion of three hours of darkness,
"My God, my God, why hast thou forsaken me?"
(Matt. 27 : 46.)   As we see him hanging here
regarded as sin by the Father, in some sense
deserted by the Father, we may form some idea of
what the Father and the Son thought of sin.   Yes,
and we can see the lengths to which sin will go.
It crucified the Lord of glory, the only good man
who ever trod the earth.

Jesus accentuated the individual man.   He discovered the worth of the soul.   In the world of
class and caste the individual is
worth little.   "How much, then, is
a man of more value than a sheep?"   The Penalty
of Sin
(Matt. 12 : 12) he asked.   It was not an idle question.   If a man is better than a sheep, respect
human rights and treat a man better than a sheep.
Is that true on your farm, in your factory, your

store, your mine, your home? Yes, and let the
man realize his own worth. Stoicism taught and
practised suicide and cheapened human life.
"What shall a man give in exchange for his
soul?" (Matt. 16 : 26.) Jesus placed the human
soul over against the whole material universe.

Moral responsibility is large in the teaching of
Christ. Guilt is written on every man's heart.
Death, spiritual death, is the condition of the
unsaved. They are dead. "Leave the dead to
bury their own dead" (Luke 9 : 60). The penalty
for guilt is inexorable. Punishment is not simply
corrective and temporary, but chiefly retributive
and eternal. God "is able to destroy both soul
and body in hell" (Matt. 10 : 28). Yes, "and
except ye repent, ye shall all likewise perish"
(Luke 13 : 5). The final punishment is eternal
with the devil and his angels. "For what shall a
man be profited, if he shall gain the whole world,
and forfeit his own life?" (Matt. 16 : 26.) That
is the point; lose *his own* soul. Lose *himself*,
Luke has it (9 : 25). The soul is the man's real
self. That is his life. It is pitiful to care so
much for the bodily life and seek to save that and
lose the real life. God is not unjust to punish
sin. Not to do so would upset the moral universe. Ethical standards would fall. There would
be no wrong nor right. Sin is eternal and relent-

less, and the punishment must be correspondingly
eternal.

Is there a remedy? "Is there a balm in Gil-
ead? Is there a physician there?" (Jer. 8 : 22.)
If so, what is the balm? The
heathen had tried philosophy, and **The Remedy**
it brought many noble ethical pre- **for Sin**
cepts and beautiful ideals. The trouble lay in the
disparity between precept and performance. The
heathen world had wandered away from God into
the Serbonian bog of polytheism. The Jews had
special leading from the hand of God, but they
too hungered for new gods. The law as peda-
gogue had with difficulty kept them in guard till
Christ, the Schoolmaster, should come. Type had
no efficacy in itself. Shadow could not act as
substance. Ceremony and ritual only symbolized
other things. There was saving truth in the Old
Testament, for the spiritual life is presented there,
and the sacrifices pointed to the great atoning
Sacrifice. But the letter finally put the spirit in
bondage. When Christ came, the Jews could not
see the spirit for the letter. They no longer saw
the spirit *in* the letter. The world was helpless
and hopeless.

Our Lord was not surprised at his death, for
he knew from the first that he must die. He had
come to die for our sins and in our stead. His

hour was ever before him. "The Son of man
must suffer many things and be slain and raised
the third day" (Luke 9 : 22). They will crucify
the Son of Man, he said. But "thus it *behooved*
the Christ to suffer and rise from the dead the
third day" (Luke 24 : 46). "Except a corn of
wheat fall into the ground and die, it abideth
alone" (John 12 : 24). "I lay down my life that
I may take it again" (John 10 : 17). He came to
give his life a ransom for many. And it will not
be in vain. "And I, if I be lifted up from the
earth, will draw all men unto me" (John 12 : 32).
"For God so loved the world that he gave his
only begotten Son that whosoever believeth in
him should not perish, but have eternal life"
(John 3 : 16). "For this cause came I unto this
hour" (John 12 : 27). "This is my blood of the
covenant, which is shed for many unto remission
of sins" (Matt. 26 : 28). "Nevertheless, not my
will, but thine be done" (Luke 22 : 42). "It is
finished" (John 19 : 30). Thus Jesus spoke of
his atoning death for human sin. Thus he won
the right to offer life to sinners on the basis of
his death.

But there is one thing more that is needed.
This atonement makes possible reconciliation with
the Father; was, indeed, prompted by the Father's
love; but actual reconciliation is not yet accom-

plished in any given case till the sinner comes back to the Father with confession of sin. The prodigal son came and said, "Father, *I have sinned*" (Luke 15 : 21). That is the hard word to say, but repentance is essential, for God will not out of hand forgive a rebellious sinner. Here we pass deeper into the mysteries of grace. The sinful soul is dead and cannot turn to God for life. Yet we must be born again or we perish, Jesus said to Nicodemus (John 3 : 3). The impulse to life must come from God who is life, and life reaches death from outside. But there must likewise be the spiritual response to the new life. The delicate spiritual process that we call regeneration from God's side and repentance or conversion from man's side is not fully unfolded. These are, however, blessed facts in the Christian's life. The essential thing for us to know is that forgiveness of sin is possible in Christ. This Jesus offers us and this we can find nowhere else. No wonder there is joy in the presence of the angels over one sinner that repents.

What is the remedy that Christ offers to a hopeless sinner? Is it a new system of doctrine? A new philosophy? A new State? A new book? A new organization? A new church? A new ritual? A new preacher? A new idea? He wrote no book. He advanced many new ideas as

others had done ; he proclaimed glorious doctrines ;
he gathered a group of disciples around him.   He
set up anew the kingdom of God.   But in none of
these plans do we find freedom from sin.   Jesus
offers himself as the Saviour from sin.   He is the
remedy.   He lived a sinless life, and offered himself as the Lamb without blemish.   He grappled
with sin at close quarters.   With a perfect life he
offered a perfect sacrifice, and the Father is well
pleased.   So the Son comes to the sinner and
offers himself as Saviour.   " Ye believe in God ;
believe also in me" (John 14 : 1).   " Come unto
me" (Matt. 11 : 28).   "And whosoever liveth and
believeth in me shall never die" (John 11 : 26).
" If the Son shall make you free, ye shall be free
indeed" (John 8 : 36).   "I came that they may
have life" (John 10 : 10).   He offers life to us
"abundantly."   We begin to live in Christ and
we go on living in Christ.   With Jesus ethical
conduct is the fruit of life, not life the fruit of
ethical precepts or conduct.   This is what sets
Jesus apart from all else.   He gives us life.   The
old flower of virtue has a new fragrance and
the fruit a new flavor, for it grows in the soil of
life, not death.

When the Greeks came to Philip and said re-
spectfully, " Sir, we would see Jesus " (John 12 :
21), Philip did not dare comply with the courteous

request. Was it regular? Was it orthodox for
Gentiles to meet Jesus? He interviewed the usually
wise Andrew on the grave problem.   It was more
than both could settle.   They came to Jesus with
this problem, but not, it seems, with the Greeks.
The soul of Jesus was greatly troubled. He did not
seek to unravel their technical pettifogging scruples.
The cross would alone break down the middle
wall of partition between Jew and Gentile.   Jesus
spoke about his death and struggled in prayer with
the Father, who heard him and spoke to comfort
him.   "And I, if I be lifted up from the earth,
will draw all men unto myself" (John 12 : 32).
When men come to us and ask for bread, do we
give them a stone?   When they seek Jesus, do
we give our theological system?   For orthodoxy,
church, preacher, the Bible itself, will be stumbling-
blocks if they come between the soul and Jesus.
"Come unto me," he said, "and I will give you
rest" (Matt. 11 : 28).

CHAPTER IV

THE KINGDOM

"Thy kingdom come" (Matt. 6 : 10).

In selecting key-words around which to group
the teachings of Jesus, the word kingdom is essential. This is the well-spring of human blessing.
After the word sin the logical and the necessary
word is the kingdom, for thus is Christ the remedy
for sin. He gives us himself and he is life. Sin
results in death and Jesus offers the water of life.
When we take him the kingdom of God enters us
and we enter it. The kingdom comes with the
King. The King comes when we let him rule
over us as Lord and Saviour.

"The kingdom of heaven is at hand" (Matt.
3 : 2), John the Baptist announced, for the King
was at hand. The King himself took
The Theme up the same cry. "Repent ye ; for
of Jesus' the kingdom of heaven is at hand"
Teaching (Matt. 4 : 17). Thus Jesus began
his Galilean ministry, vitally linking his message
with that of John the Baptist, for he said : "The
time is fulfilled" (Matt. 4 : 17 ; Mark 1 : 15).

When the Twelve were sent out on their preaching tour Jesus said : "As ye go, preach, saying, The kingdom of heaven is at hand " (Matt. 10 : 7). He laid upon his disciples the burden of proclaiming the kingdom. When the Seventy were sent forth Jesus said : "Say unto them, The kingdom of God is come nigh unto you " (Luke 10 : 9). If the message was rejected, "howbeit know this, that the kingdom of God is come nigh," even if these do reject it. " The gospel of God " is " the gospel of the kingdom." In Matthew we nearly always have the term, kingdom of heaven, but in the other Gospels, kingdom of God. In John kingdom of God occurs only twice, but in a very important connection (John 3 : 3, 5) in the conversation with Nicodemus about the new birth. Eternal life in the Gospel of John is the phrase that is equivalent to the kingdom of God in the synoptics. Such was the great theme of Jesus' preaching and teaching, a theme that quickened the pulse of every Jew who heard it discussed by the king Messiah.

In the Acts and the Epistles the expression does not occur so often as in the synoptic Gospels. It still exists and in the same sense, but is largely displaced by such **The Origin** words as gospel, salvation, faith, **of the Term** life, and church in the general sense. It is a comprehensive and unifying term for the gospel prin-

ciple and state, and was used more by Jesus than
in the apostolic time, when Christianity was more
highly organized and analyzed.   In modern times,
until lately, Christian writers have largely dis-
used it, perhaps owing to the growth of demo-
cratic ideas and an instinctive reluctance to use a
monarchical term for Christianity in its essential
idea.   The later extension of the word church in
more recent times to great general organizations
also had a tendency toward the disuse of the
term.   But new accent has now come on the
teaching of Jesus, and that accent has naturally
brought to the front again the word kingdom, for
it was the ruling word of Christ about his message.
In the Old Testament an everlasting kingdom is
promised to David.   "I will establish his kingdom.
He shall build an house for my name, and I will
establish the throne of his kingdom forever. . .
Thine house and thy kingdom shall be made sure
forever before thee."   So Nathan spoke to David.
The words were understood to mean an earthly
monarchy that took the place of the theocracy that
had existed till Saul was made king in answer to
the clamor of the people (2 Sam. 7 : 13, 16).   Even
in Ps. 89 it is not clear that it is a spiritual kingdom whose perpetuity is guaranteed.   "I have
sworn unto David my servant.   Thy seed will
I establish forever and build up thy throne to all

generations" (Ps. 89 : 3 f.).   In Dan. 7 : 14, 18, 27 this everlasting kingdom is promised to the saints, who will come from all nations and tongues.   It is thus a universal kingdom and not merely one composed of Jews.   It is universal, and not merely Jewish.   There is thus a gradual expansion in the use of the term till we find it in the mouth of John the Baptist and Jesus as the comprehensive term for the work and rule of God in the hearts of men. With John and Jesus the term kingdom has the spiritual, not the national, idea.   It is worth noting that nearly all the distinctive words used by Jesus in Matt. 16 : 18 occur in Ps. 89, though not in exactly the same sense.   Thus we have "build" in Ps. 89 : 4, "ecclesia" in ver. 5, "Christos" in ver. 38, "hades" in ver. 48.   The theme is the same, the perpetuity of the kingdom ; the one Davidic, the other Messianic.

We must take all the senses of the word or else make exceptions.   As Jesus used it, kingdom means essentially the reign of God in the heart.   Sometimes the idea **Various Senses of the Word** is possession or kingly authority or kingship ; sometimes the idea is rather that of the subjects of the rule of God, but never does Jesus use it in the sense of territory or country.   He does not seem to have the idea of organization in the word as was common in other connections (Matt.

12 : 25). Sometimes two concepts will be present at once, as authority and rule, or rule and the subjects. Reign is the best single English equivalent, but the world has become familiar with the term kingdom. In the Old Testament theocracy God is king of the Jews in the literal sense of earthly ruler, for they had no other king. After Saul was made king God is still the king in the higher spiritual sense, and the people who serve him are the subjects of his kingdom. There was thus a phrase ready at hand for our Master's use. So likewise the word Israel had developed from the literal sense to the spiritual also.

The Assyrian and the Babylonian captivity inaugurated a long period of servitude for the Jews. Save during the glorious Maccabean era they never recovered independence. Hence the literal kingdom of the Jews did cease. The hope of national independence then became the guiding star in Jewish politics and theology. This hope appears in the numerous Jewish writings of the time, especially in the apocalypses. After the Romans overcame the Jews, freedom from Roman rule centered in the coming of the Messiah. The Messianic hope of the Old Testament prophets turned to a glorious Jewish king who should set up his kingdom in Jerusalem, drive out the

The Popular Jewish Idea of the Kingdom

Romans and conquer the world, and introduce a millennium by making all men Jews. This was the teaching of the Jews of the time. The greater the oppression of their enemies became, the more strongly this hope seized the Pharisees and the masses. When John the Baptist proclaimed on the banks of the Jordan, " Repent, for the kingdom of heaven is at hand " (Matt. 3 : 2), this is what the people understood him to mean. The hour for Jewish deliverance had arrived. The Messiah was now at hand to restore Israel to its pristine glory and to spread Judaism all over the world. Certainly John the Baptist had no such narrow idea of the kingdom of God. " Repent," he said, not " Gather an army." John was a student of the Old Testament rather than of rabbinical theology, and his teaching is in the spirit and power of the Old Testament prophets, of whom he was the last. And he was full of the Holy Spirit. He was the herald of the kingdom, and spoke just before the full fruition of his own glorious words. He surpasses us in inherent greatness, but we surpass him in richness of opportunity. He was in the dawn and we are in the day. He had God's message *for* the times, not merely man's message *from* the times. John understood the nature of the Messianic kingdom and Jesus did not teach a Pharisaic kingdom.

Was there no kingdom of God before Jesus began to preach ? Surely so, but the rule of God in the hearts of men was on such a limited scale before this time, that in a true sense the kingdom could be said to begin with Jesus. The new epoch in the kingdom amounted in effect to a new start. "The law and the prophets were until John" (Luke 16 : 16). He was a great milepost in God's dealings with men. The shadow came before, but now the King himself is here, for Jesus as well as the Father is king in the kingdom. Hence John announced that the kingdom of God was at hand because the King had come.

When Did the Kingdom Begin?

It is thus that Jesus himself spoke of the kingdom as still future in one sense. We shall discuss this point directly. But he also spoke of it as a present realization, as here already in the hearts of men, as the glorious fulfilment of God's promise to men, the long-expected Messianic dispensation. Hence he said that it was at hand, had in fact come already to some, was a ready blessing for all who would open their hearts to the King. The fact that Jesus was casting out demons by the Spirit of God was proof that the kingdom of God was already come (Matt. 12 : 28). The kingdom comes not as a great governmental organization is set up over men. The rather does the kingdom

come with men one by one and spreads from soul
to soul as the torch of the kingdom is passed on.
Now at last the fire of God was burning in some
souls, a fire that would burn on through the ages
with mighty power. The kingdom of God had
come among men. Some, though timid like Joseph
of Arimathea, were yet "looking for the kingdom
of God" (Mark 15 : 43). Others, though not far
from the kingdom (Mark 12 : 34) may never have
entered in.

It is the kingdom of heaven, of God, the rule of
God in the heart. It was a woful disappointment
to the Jews to learn that Jesus was
only going to establish a spiritual **What Sort**
kingdom with a spiritual king, and **of a Kingdom**
not an actual, visible rule in Jeru- **Is It?**
salem. Satan had offered to make Jesus king of
all the kingdoms of the world with all their glory.
It was a fascinating temptation. Once the people,
in a frenzy of enthusiasm beside the sea of Galilee,
tried to make him go to Jerusalem and set up such
a kingdom (John 6 : 15). We will "make" him
king, they cried. But Jesus listened to God rather
than to Satan and the people. He pushed both
temptations from him, a thing that those religious
leaders have not done who have combined Church
and State from the days of Constantine, till Roger
Williams proclaimed religious liberty for all men.

The great ecclesiastical machine at Rome contro-
verts the fundamental conceptions of Christ, that
the kingdom is invisible and spiritual, not a temporal and visible organization.   The Pharisees
grew impatient with Jesus, and wished to force his
hand about the kingdom and asked " when the
kingdom of God cometh."   His answer is significant for all time: " The kingdom of God cometh
not with observation : neither shall they say, Lo,
here! or, There! for lo, the kingdom of God is
within you" (Luke 17 : 20 f.).   So the correct
translation, not "among you."   In one of the Oxy-
rhynchus Sayings of Jesus exactly this construction
occurs where the context makes "the kingdom of
heaven within you" necessary.   "You" here does
not have to mean the unsaved Pharisees, but only
those in whom the kingdom of God actually exists.
In the mind of Christ the kingdom has a spiritual
content.   It is related to repentance and is a spiritual experience.   In a word, the kingdom of God
signifies to a man the entrance upon and the enjoyment of eternal life.   He carries the kingdom of
God in his own bosom.   He is enveloped in the
riches of the reign of God.   It is, indeed, God's
good pleasure to give us the kingdom (Luke
12 : 32); he has given us the very keys of the
kingdom (Matt. 16 : 19), but in giving us the kingdom he has given us the bread of heaven, not

earthly or ecclesiastical power. We have seen the
kingdom come in power (Mark 9 : 1), but it is the
power of the Holy Spirit, not of human authority.
There are greater and less in the kingdom of God,
but not as John and James supposed (Matt. 20 : 21).
The high place will belong to him who is most
like the Master in the spirit of service (Matt.
5 : 19; 18 : 1, 4). This one is alone great in the
kingdom of God.

In giving the characteristics of those who are
in the kingdom, in what we call the Beatitudes
at the beginning of the Sermon on the Mount
(Matt. 5 : 3–12), Jesus laid emphasis on the inner
state of the heart as the true source of happiness.
" Happy are the poor in spirit" ; " happy are they
that hunger and thirst after righteousness";
" happy are the pure in heart," he said. It was a
revolutionary and incomprehensible idea to the
sacramental Pharisee and the materialistic Roman
and intellectual Greek. Nobody thought this was
happiness and few wanted it. But this is the
very essence of Christianity. It does bring peace
and happiness to the heart and so to the man, for
the soul is the man. " Seek ye *first* the kingdom
of God " (Matt. 6 : 33), said Jesus. This is the
primal thing in time and rank. First the kingdom, then the righteousness; first the kingdom,
then earthly good. First the kingdom, then the

local church.   If no kingdom there is no use
for the local church.   This is what we call a regenerated church-membership.   The local church
is the great God-appointed agency for the spread
of the kingdom, but it is not the kingdom and is
not equal to the kingdom (not one and not all local
churches).   Jesus did not establish local churches
as divine institutions, and then save people so that
the churches could have members in them.   He
saved people, put the kingdom of God in them,
and then put them in local churches to go to work
for God.   The local church is a regiment in the
army and may have traitors in it.   It is a fighting
machine to fight the devil, however, and not believers.   The kingdom is the cause for which the
local churches battle.   The kingdom, then, is composed of all the saved who are ruled by Christ the
Lord and who serve him.

It is not strange that the words of Jesus were
perverted by his enemies.   These very men who
should have been able to lead men into the kingdom, not simply were blind themselves to spiritual
light, but they hindered those who wished to find
God.   They shut the door of the kingdom of
heaven before men (Matt. 23 : 14).   This is the
pathos and the pity of the situation.   The ac-
credited guides of heaven had become stumbling-
blocks to keep people out of heaven   Jesus had

to reach the people of the time over the heads of the religious teachers and even in opposition to them. They were angry with him for not being a temporal king, and so before Pilate they charged him with making himself a king as a rival to Cæsar, the very thing that they were angry with him for not doing. Poor Pilate was hopelessly befuddled when Jesus said : " My kingdom is not of this world " (John 18 : 36). His kingdom was that of truth and did not encroach on the realm of Cæsar. Even the disciples could not comprehend it. " Unto you is given the mystery of the kingdom of God" (Mark 4 : 11), but it was hard for them to see into the mystery. Even just before the ascension of Christ they will say : " Lord, dost thou at this time restore the kingdom to Israel ? " (Acts 1 : 6.) It is not until the great Pentecost that the disciples will fully understand, but after that day they will joyfully proclaim the kingdom of God to men.

The self-complacent Pharisees thought that the kingdom of God belonged to them by right of inheritance. "We have Abraham to our Father" (Matt. 3 : 9). It was **How Does** incomprehensible and revolutionary **One Enter the** to be told by both John and Jesus **Kingdom?** that they should "repent." They listened eagerly to the statement that the kingdom of God was at hand, but failed to grasp the spiritual and ethical significance of its necessary condition. And even in our English translation we have an unfortunate rendition in "repent," a word that accents an emotion connected with this profound spiritual revolution rather than the spiritual change itself. The scribe should be instructed in the kingdom of God (Matt. 13 : 52). Nicodemus failed utterly to understand the fundamental words of Jesus : "Except a man be born anew (or from above), he cannot see the kingdom of God" (John 3 : 3). The new birth is not only essential to entrance into the kingdom, but the new birth is of heavenly origin and is spiritual in character. Paradoxical as it may appear, the only way for us to enter the kingdom is for the kingdom to enter us. The kingdom of God is within us. The kingdom comes in with the King. May we let the King come in and rule our hearts. When we let God into our hearts, then the kingdom comes to us and we enter it. We come in as little children with the spirit of childlike trust and simplicity, for of such is the kingdom (Mark 10 : 14). Simplicity and singleness characterize the child's entrance into the kingdom. Hence the child is the type. There will, of course, be earnestness, for "the kingdom of heaven suffereth violence and the violent take it by force" (Matt. 11 : 12). And no wonder, if

men only knew that it is better to enter the
kingdom of God lame and halt than with both
feet and both hands to go to hell (Mark 9 : 47).
It is hard for some men to get into the kingdom,
for they wish to carry their sins with them. The
rich, especially, find it difficult, as hard as for a
camel to go through the eye of a needle. That is,
with men it is impossible for rich men to be saved.
But with God all things are possible and there is
hope for them (Matt. 19 : 26). But Jesus did not
mean by this to say that the poor man would find
the door of heaven open to him because he was
poor. Lazarus is not in Abraham's bosom because
he is poor. Some will be not far from the kingdom and yet may turn back (Mark 12 : 34), and
the one who looks back is not fit for the kingdom.
Not every one that thought he was in the kingdom
would realize this greatest blessing. " Not every
one that saith Lord, Lord, shall enter the kingdom" (Matt. 7 : 21). There will be surprises in
heaven. Indeed, said Jesus, the righteousness of
men must exceed that of the scribes and the
Pharisees, else they would in no case enter the
kingdom (Matt. 5 : 20), for the very harlots go
into the kingdom of God before them (Matt. 21 :
31), so hard was it for the Jewish ecclesiastical
leaders to realize their own sinfulness. But to this
day it is difficult for men to apprehend the true

spiritual value of Christianity apart from ecclesias-
ticism and ceremonialism.   To establish this conception cost Jesus the hate of the Pharisees.   To
maintain it meant the death of Stephen and for
Paul the battle of his life.   To restore it and pre-
serve it is the true Protestant principle.   This vital
conception of Christianity can only survive as one
sees Christ as the revelation of the Father.

It is both present and future.   The reign of
God is already in the hearts of men.   The kingdom
is realized whenever and wherever
Is the King- a sinner turns to Christ for salva-
dom Present tion and finds him.   " Repent, for
or Future ? the kingdom of God is at hand "
(Matt. 3 : 2).   It dawns with the new birth and
repentance.   And yct Jesus spoke also of the kingdom coming in the future.   He spoke thus : " Till
they see the kingdom of God come " (Mark 9 : 1);
" till I drink it anew in the kingdom " ; " till it be
fulfilled in the kingdom of God " (Luke 22 : 16, 18).
The fulness and the richness of the reign of God
are still ahead of us.   In heaven above we shall sit
down with Jesus in the full glory of God's rule, or
kingdom.   We shall see Abraham in the kingdom of God (Luke 13 : 28).   Till then the kingdom is coming more and more.   It is gratuitous to
charge Jesus with inconsistency and incoherence,
because he had two points of view concerning the

kingdom. Language is not a perfect expression of ideas, and it is very common for words to have a larger and a smaller content. One can use a term now in the full and now in the narrower sense, and trust to the common sense of people to see the difference. But for this, speech would be, indeed, the art of concealing thought. The kingdom of God will not be fully come till the struggle with sin is over and all the elect are gathered to the King. Then the kingdom will be wholly in heaven. Till then the kingdom of God is on earth and in heaven, present and future, come and coming.

The wonderful parables of the kingdom set forth the origin, character, and final consummation of the kingdom. There are chiefly three groups of them as spoken by Jesus, two in Matthew (and Mark) and one in Luke. The kingdom of heaven is like, said Jesus, the grain of mustard seed in its small beginning and great destiny ; like the leaven in the meal in its pervasive and intensive power ; like the pearl in its preciousness ; like the hid treasure in arousing interest ; like the sower sowing seed in that some seed is blessed and some is not ; like the silent and wondrous growth of the grain by night in its mystery and power ; like the field that contains wheat and tares, or the net with fishes good and bad, in that the kingdom exists in a world full of sin and where the evil one is active. But in the midst of sin the kingdom grows, overcoming sin, driving it out here and there, spreading the power of Christ. It is slow work, but it is sure work. The kingdom is not the world, nor of the world, but in the world. The kingdom is here to transform the world and restore it to Christ. But some tares will grow in the midst of the wheat to the end. But they will still be tares and will be separated then, not now. The field where the kingdom works is the world, but Satan is busy in the same field. This slow expansion of the kingdom of God during the Christian centuries is one of the most magnificent things in history. The mustard seed has spread its branches all over the world. The leaves of the tree of life have fallen among all nations. Jesus followed the law of life and not of mechanical contrivance. He implanted spiritual life in the hearts of some men and this life has reproduced itself by the Holy Spirit in spite of all opposition. The kingdom of God is to-day the most vital reality of earth. No man can touch it, for it is like life. And yet, like life, it is indestructible. The laws of the kingdom are immutable and inscrutable. No one knows how the blade of corn grows nor how the kingdom of God vitalizes sinful hearts into life. But we rejoice in the presence of the supreme fact of the majesty and magnitude of the kingdom on earth to-day, the power that makes for righteousness.

The kingdom of God would be taken from the Jews because they were not worthy, Jesus said (Matt. 21 : 43), but the kingdom itself would go on and increase in power. Some of the so-called sons of the kingdom will never see it. This was a mighty revolution to take the kingdom of God away from the Jews. The apostolic history answers this prophecy and so does modern history. It goes from nation to nation. It is an eternal kingdom and was prepared before the foundation of the world (Matt. 25 : 34). In Dan. 7 : 27 it is called an everlasting kingdom, in accordance with the promise to David. And Jesus, apparently with this glorious promise in mind, interpreted in the Messianic sense, and especially as set forth in Ps. 89, said to Peter that the gates of hades should not prevail against his church. The kingdom bears no direct parallel to the local churches, for all members of the local churches are not members of the kingdom. They should be, to be sure, for we should have a regenerated local church-membership, but that is not always the actual fact. So apparently what Jesus in Matt. 16 : 18 calls "my church," in the next verse he calls "the kingdom," whose

The Permanence of the Kingdom

keys he gives to Peter and to every preacher and teacher of the gospel of the kingdom who opens the door of salvation to the unsaved. The gates of hades shall not prevail against the kingdom of Christ. This parallel between the general sense of church and the kingdom applies to only one sense of kingdom, that of the subjects of the rule of God. This seems to be the case here, though it is used in other ways not applicable to the general sense of the word church. One sense of church and one sense of kingdom are co-extensive. This great temple has been steadily rising all over the world, the spiritual house of God (1 Peter 2 : 5). It is the stone cut out of the mountain that will overturn and overturn.

Satan offered Christ a short and easy road to the conquest of the world. He showed him all the kingdoms of the world and the **The Final Victory of the Kingdom** glory of them. "All these will I give thee, if thou wilt fall down and worship me" (Matt. 4 : 9). That was all ; just acknowledge the sovereignty and power of Satan and there would be no conflict. This is always the plea of the compromiser. But Jesus chose the hard and the long road that led to the cross. He would found his kingdom in his heart's blood and in the love of the children of God. This would bring sacrifice and humiliation for him

and ceaseless struggle till final victory should come.
But he would win in the end. The time will come
when the kingdoms of the world have become the
kingdom of our Lord and his Christ (Rev. 11 : 15).
That will be heaven indeed. We shall then see
the Son of Man come in his kingdom (Matt.
16 : 28). Then we shall eat and drink with him
(Luke 22 : 30). This kingdom was prepared for
us from before the foundation of the world (Matt.
25 : 34), and we shall realize our inheritance with
Jesus in heaven. Jesus saw the victory before it
comes. He had the sublime faith, the opti-
mistic vision to see beyond the grave, beyond the
long conflict with Satan, to the full and final tri-
umph in the end, when the redeemed shall be
gathered together as wheat out of the tares. It is
the privilege of the believer to catch the enthusiasm
of this hope and to share in the struggle for this
glorious end. Till then our work is to battle with
Satan, as did Jesus and as does Jesus now, for in
heaven he is still our Captain, leading the hosts on
earth through the Holy Spirit and planning the
greatest campaign of the ages, the campaign of
righteousness against sin. The kingdom of God is
in deadly conflict with the kingdom of Satan.
" Lo, I am with you all the days " (Matt. 28 : 20).
He is leading us to victory. " Then shall the
righteous shine forth as the sun in the kingdom of

the Father" (Matt. 13 : 43). Here is the main-spring in missionary endeavor, the sure final victory of light over darkness, of Christ over Satan.

It is not bounded by race ties nor by national lines. They shall come from the East and from the West, from the North and from the South, and sit down in the kingdom (Matt. 8 : 11). The individual is the unit in the kingdom. It is composed of redeemed individuals, not of local churches, not of denominations, not of nations, not of races. In Christ Jesus there is no difference, and Christ is all and in all. As the individual is the unit, so the ultimate responsibility rests on the individual. The local church should work for the spread of the kingdom. That is what it exists for. But a sleepy or dead church does not absolve the individual Christian from responsibility. The complacent report of a dead church to the district Association cannot release a live Christian from his duty. The standard of duty in the work of the kingdom is the ideal of Christ for each of us. But those who come from North and East, South and West, will all come in the same way. Jesus is the way to the Father, and there is no private door into the kingdom, save through him. "Are there few that be saved?" (Luke 13 : 23 f.). That question was asked Jesus, and his answer was for men to strive themselves to enter in by the narrow door. The problem for each of us is to find God the Father through Christ the Son, and thus receive life, and that abundantly. And it is a personal problem. The kingdom has a social side, but only as individuals are reached. A regenerated society is the goal, and comes only by saving individuals. We shall hasten the kingdom of God, just as we realize the kingdom ourselves, and seek to win other individuals to the service of God. That is the secret. Eternal life is the possession of every believer, whether Jew or Gentile. Let the King come in his beauty and let us greet him in the way. If this view of the kingdom sounds like Utopia it is possible in Christ. If we are to enjoy the kingdom of God in heaven we must enjoy the kingdom of heaven here. Jesus taught us to pray: "Thy kingdom come; thy will be done, as in heaven, so on earth" (Matt. 6 : 10). We should help answer our own prayer for the spread of the kingdom of God. So shall we realize the highest good for ourselves and for the world.

CHAPTER V

"Do not your righteousness before men" (Matt. 6 : 1).

DOCTOR STALKER says that in the mouth of Jesus righteousness carries the same idea that virtue did with the ancients, only it is higher. The world has too high an idea of sin and too low an idea of righteousness. Jesus uses the word virtue not at all, but the idea pervades all he says. He uses the word righteous or righteousness seldom, yet it is just this rectitude that he sought to create in us. Character is our modern word for it, as Doctor Stalker says, but here again we do not find that Jesus ever used such a word. The righteous man, ὁ δίκαιος, was the man who walked in the way pointed out by God to be correct. In this sense Zacharias and Elisabeth were called "righteous before God" (Luke 1 : 6), without meaning to claim sinlessness for them, but only uprightness of character. Salvation by character is not taught by Christ, though high character is just what he seeks to create in men. He gradually perfects in us real likeness to himself.

78

This is clearly what Jesus had in mind as the subject of the greatest of his discourses. "Except your righteousness shall exceed the righteousness of the scribes and Pharisees, ye shall in no wise enter into the kingdom of heaven" (Matt. 5 : 20). "Your righteousness" is the thing that he is after. "Blessed are they that hunger and thirst after righteousness" (Matt. 5 : 6), he had just said, "for they shall be filled." It is possible to obtain this righteousness; nay, those who hunger after it will get it. By righteousness Jesus means righteous living and not justification. It is sanctification as set forth in Rom. 6–8, rather than justification, as expounded in Rom. 3–5. Practical righteousness is the theme of the Epistle of James and is emphasized in the preaching of John the Baptist. But it is a practical righteousness that is the fruit of the spiritual life. It may be well to sketch in outline this great sermon so as to catch its spirit, since the larger part of Christ's teaching on righteousness is contained in it.

The Theme of the Sermon on the Mount

The introduction (Matt. 5 : 3–16; Luke 6 : 20–26) shows the character of people who are in the kingdom of heaven. Spiritual qualities are emphasized entirely, such as longing, humility, purity, etc. The theme of the discourse (Matt. 5 : 17–20) is the righteousness brought in by the kingdom of

heaven as superior to that of the rabbinical teachers. The rest of the sermon, save the end, is
argument and illustration of this proposition (Matt.
5 : 21 to 7 : 12 ; Luke 6 : 31, 36–42)

The conclusion (Matt. 7 : 13–29; Luke
6 : 43–49) presents the final test at the judgment to be the righteousness wrought out in the
heart and life. Righteousness is the fruit of the
kingdom and is the proof of the kingdom.

To the people at the time it was revolutionary.
They had never heard spiritual morality put thus
before—so genuine, so inward, so
vital, so profound, so noble, so ideal.
Here was the breath of heaven and
not the pottering inanities of the
scribes, the spiritual teachers of the
time. It is not true that it is merely ethical with
no spiritual basis. The Beatitudes precede the
discussion of practical morality, and this inward
state is what makes it possible for men to exceed
the righteousness of scribe and Pharisee. Seek
ye first his kingdom, and his righteousness
(Matt. 6 : 33). The kingdom comes before the
righteousness and makes possible the righteousness. It is impossible to reach the height of this
sermon. The modern teachers of ethics often
affect indifference to the teaching of Jesus, because he did not put his ideas in scientific phrase.

The
Significance
of Christ's
Teaching About
Righteousness

It is a pitiful business, for Jesus is the greatest teacher of ethics of all the ages. This discourse itself makes an epoch in ethical conceptions. Jesus took ethics out of the clouds and brought it down to earth. He injected life into the ideas of morality. He transmutes ideal into real by the alembic of the Spirit. With Christ the new heart stands before righteousness. The new life begins with the new birth. The roots of righteousness strike down into the renewed spirit of man. This is the man who builds his house upon the rock. This house, and this alone, will stand.

The scribe was purely legal. He held to the letter of the law. The scribe accepted the Old Testament in a literal sense and added to it the traditions of the elders, making a second Bible more important in their minds than the first. The scribe confined murder to the outward act; Jesus found murder in the heart, in the anger that led to it. The modern judge and jury often cannot find it anywhere. The scribe saw adultery only in the actual crime; Jesus saw it even in the licentious look. The scribe confined profanity to violent oaths; Jesus insisted on the absence of superfluous exaggerations. The scribe taught the letter of the law as to retaliation; Jesus taught forbearance

against resentful vengeance. The scribe taught
hate of one's enemy; Jesus taught love of our
enemies. The spirit was in the letter of the Old
Testament, but the scribe made it imposible to
get at the spirit for the letter. No wonder that
Jesus charged the lawyers (scribes) with taking
the key of knowledge and locking the door and
throwing the key away. Rabbinical theology is
a synonym for hair-splitting, but they have no
monopoly of the art. They would not go in themselves, nor would they let others in. Certainly
the scribes were not hungering and thirsting after
righteousness. They trusted in themselves that
they were righteous, for they were usually Pharisees (Luke 18 : 9). Hence when Jesus denounced
the Pharisees at a feast the scribes (lawyers) took
it as personal offense (Luke 11 : 37–54). The
Master, to be impartial, gave the scribes an equal
number of woes. The scribes were a professional
class ; the Pharisees were a party.

The Pharisees were advocates of ceremonial
righteousness. The outward, the sacramental, was
all-important. But the trouble al-
The
Righteousness
of the Pharisee
ways is that the insistence on the
external will lead to hypocrisy.
Ceremonial righteousness, when
merely ceremonial, spells hypocritical righteousness, which is the worst form of unrighteousness.

The world hates cant and indorses the judgment of Christ. In hell the lowest place will be occupied by the hypocrite who fleeced pious people under the guise of Christianity. The Pharisee wished to get *credit* for being righteous. Else what was the use of being good? He did not think that virtue was its own reward, but wished a reward for being good. "Take heed that ye do not your righteousness before men, to be seen of them" (Matt. 6 : 1). Thus he gave alms to get glory of men. If he had lived now his gifts would always be in the papers, religious and otherwise. Thus he prayed on the street corners to be seen of men. Thus he fasted with a long countenance to be seen of men to fast. Thus the Pharisees kept one eye on heaven and the other to the main chance on earth. Thus they sought to serve God and Mammon. Thus they criticised their neighbors with pious innocence and gratitude. So the proud hypocrite stood in the temple and prayed with himself, not with God. He did not need anything, but gave the Lord some valuable information about his own graces and glories. It was on the scribes and Pharisees both that Jesus poured out the vials of his wrath in the twenty-third chapter of Matthew, the fiercest philippic of all history. Each time he called them "hypocrites," and, as Doctor Stalker has said, since then hypocrisy has been regarded as the meanest of sins. They stand in the way of the kingdom, then and now. They make their proselytes worse than before, and they are already sons of hell. They are blind hair-splitters, showing how to swear and not sin. They lay wrong emphasis on relatively unimportant things, straining out gnats and swallowing camels, big camels with numerous humps. They care more for the outside of the cup than for what is in the cup. It is all-important to them to keep up appearances, even if they steal to do it. They are like whited sepulchres, whitewashed tombstones. "Even so ye also outwardly appear righteous unto men, but inwardly ye are full of hypocrisy and iniquity." Ye are like your fathers. "Ye serpents, ye generation of vipers, how shall ye escape the judgment of hell?" Note the withering scorn of it all. Jesus is the eternal foe of Pharisaism, ancient and modern, the holier-than-thou man, the professional holiness man, the pretender, the sham, the fraud, the religious humbug. Let his blistering words forever burn the cheeks of those who in modern time prattle the jargon of intellectual and verbal orthodoxy, but whose hearts are heretical and whose lives reek with impurity. The Pharisee has not passed away, nor will he so long as sin remains. It is a continual temptation to take the hull for the kernel.

The Sadducee probably means the merely righteous man. He prides himself on his intellectual
superiority. He recoiled from the
noisy Pharisee with all his airs and
pretensions and traditions. He said
the Pharisee in the end would purify
the sun. And that has spots! He was simply
righteous himself. He it was that Jesus had
specially in mind when he said: "I came not
to call the righteous, but sinners" (Matt. 9 : 13).
Not that Jesus admitted the reality of this claim,
but he simply took the Sadducee at his own
estimate of himself, which was exceedingly high,
and treated him so for the moment. The market value of the Sadducees was bullish, they
being judges. If our own price was the market
value we might many of us bring a good round
sum. The Sadducee did not have much theology.
Some people now think it a virtue to be ignorant
of theology. They are very virtuous. The Sadducee chiefly denied the affirmations of the Pharisees about the resurrection, future life, and angels.
He was content with the five books of Moses,
especially his own interpretation of them. He
was the moralist of the time, who cared little for
creed and much for deed, especially his own,
judged by his own standards. The Sadducee rejoiced in pride of intellect and influential position.

The
Sadducees and
Righteousness

Jesus lifted the whole question of virtue out of the perfunctory and theoretical into the actual and the practical.   He had a theory of righteousness, but it differed wholly from the current notions. It was becoming to him and us to to fulfil all righteousness (Matt. 3 : 15), so he said when explaining why he submitted to baptism at the hands of John the Baptist.   It was a righteous thing to obey the command of God through John, even when Jesus himself had no sins of which to repent.   He could not in his own case symbolize death to sin and resurrection to newness of life by the water burial.   With Jesus righteousness is spiritual and inward.   Out of the heart are the issues of life.   The seat of the ethical life is the inner man.   The other teachers of ethics had seen this, but none had ever grasped it in all its bearings as had Jesus.   The ethical problem is immeasurably complicated by the fact that, even as children, we are by nature sinful.   The most solemn word in modern science is heredity.   Training can do much and we should use it eagerly.   But we wofully deceive ourselves if we fail to see the need of a new heart, of new life, as the basis for righteousness.

Jesus teaches inherited sin in man.   This does not mean that children dying before responsibility

Christ's Conception of Righteousness

are lost.   Far from it.   Environment cannot explain the fact that all men are bad if children are naturally good.   We are by nature sinful. Environment and culture do not eliminate the sinful nature.   The blood of Christ alone cleanses from sin through the Holy Spirit.   When God calls man or child he must answer.   That answer is conversion.   The child and the man must *come* to Jesus, for both need to come.   Thank God it is easier for the child to come.   Let him come.   How does a child receive the kingdom of God?   He just takes it with simplicity.   So we must become as little children in simple receptiveness.   Jesus put love to God and man as the prime principle of human duty.   The Old Testament does the same, but Jesus sharpened the point and emphasized the relation between love to God and love to man. This is the sum of human duty, to love.   This is duty, and duties grow out of it.   To love God is first, but to love man follows as a necessity.   To love God and not man is to be merely theological without heart and with no helping hand.   To love man and not God is to be merely humanitarian and to run the risk of not being that long.   The motive power is too slight and soon gives out. To love man is the second commandment and not the first.   It takes both to fulfil Christ's idea of human duty.   Both are essential with Jesus and

in the right order.   The Christian's humanitarian
effort is permanent, because it is rooted in love to
God.   Hence the persistence in the missionary
movement.

With Jesus righteousness is personal.   He
preaches civic righteousness surely, and often
speaks of the heathen nations or the Gentiles by
way of reproof to the Jews and the disciples.
Social righteousness is strongly emphasized by
Christ.   Modern sociology has not gone in vain to
the teaching of Jesus for light.   Several new books
have recently appeared on the social teaching of
Jesus.   This is all true.   Nowhere is the peril of
riches so revealed as in the teaching of Christ.
The sympathy of Jesus with the downtrodden
classes is genuine and strong.   He dares to be a
friend of publicans and sinnners, the worst classes
of the day.   But he never lowered himself to the
level of these classes, nor did they mistake his
purpose to help and elevate them.   Jesus understood the hollowness of the professional religious
teachers of the time and denounced them as a
class.   But none the less Christ held men indi-
vidually responsible for their sins.   One of the
great contributions of Christ to the civilization of
the world is the discovery of the individual.   The
worth of the soul is what dignifies man.   " What
shall a man give in exchange for his soul ? "   That

question rings on through the strife of class with class. Jesus came to seek and to save the lost. And he searches for the lost man by man. " He that believeth hath eternal life." The moral response to the appeal of Christ comes out of the man's inner nature, not out of any class conditions. Christ's way to lift up a class of men is to lift up the individuals in the class. Lazarus is finally in Abraham's bosom, not because he is a poor man, but because he trusted God. The rich man in the same parable is in hades in torment not because he was rich, but because he was wicked and sinful.

With Jesus righteousness is character. Character is inward, but it finds expression in the outward life which is, in fact, proof of the inner life. "By their fruits ye shall know them," Jesus urged. It is futile to call a tree good if the fruit is bad. A good tree "cannot" bring forth evil fruit. The tree is known by its fruit. You can tell an apple from a persimmon. This applies to the *kind* of fruit, and so to the general run of the Christian's life. There will be imperfect, even rotten fruit on an otherwise good tree. Fields will vary in their yield, but good soil will make *some* yield. It is the one who *hears* and *does* the sayings of Christ, whose house is built on the rock. Christ put accent on creed, but not mere belief in a

creed. Trust in God, trust in Christ, not in a
creed or system of faith.   Creed comes before
deed, but the deed should be forthcoming. Creed
is the intellectual expression of character and the
character is the crown of the creed. Character
is what Jesus wishes. He came not to make men
orthodox. That is an idle purpose in itself. He
came to make men *good*. Goodness in life starts
with right connection with God. Faith *without*
works is dead, said James.   So said Jesus, so
said Paul.

With Jesus character determines destiny. "Not
every one that saith unto me, Lord, Lord, shall
enter the kingdom of heaven" (Matt. 7 : 21).   It
is easy for some men to " say." Profession comes
easy with the flippant and the mercurial tempera-
ment. " He that doeth the will of my Father in
heaven," he it is who shall enter the kingdom of
heaven at last. This final test of character does
not destroy the force of Christ's teaching that we
must be born again, must repent or be converted.
It is impossible to do the will of God without a
new heart. But then the supreme proof of the
new heart is the desire to do God's will. Moreover, the attempt to do God's will increases our
knowledge of the teaching. " If any man willeth to
do his will, he shall know of the teaching " (John
7 : 17).   In the end of the day we must be good.

Every man has his own standard of righteousness. Every age, every nation, has its standard of righteousness. Ethical teachers have flourished in all ages, philosophical and practical. Some of these teachers affect to ignore Jesus because of his terminology. The conscience itself records varying verdicts of right or wrong, according to the light at hand. But Jesus has given us the absolute standard of righteousness. He warned the men of his time against seeking to please men. God is the one whose favor we seek. We must come up to God's idea and ideal. This is a discouraging truth at first. We know how impossible it is for us to satisfy our own standards of right, not to mention that of God. We must stand in the white light of Christ's purity and at last measure up to his image.

Varying Standards of Righteousness

There is hope for us. Jesus offers to give us the righteousness which he demands. This is his chief merit as an ethical teacher. It is not only the highest ethics, but it is possible ethics. If he asks for a wedding garment he offers it freely to all who will take it. But this righteousness by faith was a stumbling-block to the Jew and foolishness to the Greek. He offers himself as the water of life for the thirsty, the

Our Hope for Attaining to Christ's Righteousness

bread of life to the hungry, the rest for the weary, righteousness for the sinful. He demands perfect righteousness; he offers to make us so. He proposes to put a new heart in us to begin with. Else it would be a useless task.

The world's ethical teachers begin at the wrong end. With the new heart Jesus will work toward the restoration of the image of God. He will not leave us without help in that struggle. The Holy Spirit carries on the work of redemption, and completes the sanctifying process, till we shall at last be pure in heart and so can see God, for without holiness none shall see God. In the end of the day the righteousness of Christ will have displaced our filthy rags, and we shall be clothed in the blood-washed robes of the joyful throng who sing the song of Moses and the Lamb. If at first we merely put on as a new garment the righteousness of God in Christ, at last we shall be like the garment in which we are clothed. That is our destiny. For that we can hope. To that end we may toil. We shall be good, rescued from the power of Satan, the taint of Satan's rule washed away by the cleansing blood of Jesus, new hearts given us by the Holy Spirit, new characters achieved by the help of the same Spirit, and finally new bodies for our spirits. So shall we be fitted for the home on high, to live with God.

CHAPTER VI

THE HOLY SPIRIT

"He shall glorify me, for he shall take of mine and shall declare it unto you" (John 16 : 14).

SOME may wonder why the discussion of the teaching of Jesus concerning the Holy Spirit has been deferred to this point. Why was it not discussed after the chapter on the Son? That was a possible method, but it has seemed best to pursue the method of Christ himself and take up the treatment of the Holy Spirit in the historical order of the Master's own teaching. This is the order of fact and we get thus a better standpoint. We need that standpoint to apprehend this vital subject.

It was right at the very end of the life of Jesus that he spoke most about the Holy Spirit. This is natural, because it was then that the Lord's thoughts turned chiefly **The Place of** on the future of the kingdom. And **the Holy Spirit** yet there is not wanting earlier **in Christ's** teaching about the Spirit in the **Teaching** words of Jesus. It is in the Gospel of John that the later teaching chiefly occurs, while the earlier

is more generally in the Synoptics. It is notice-
able how little teaching we have from Christ about
the Holy Spirit in comparison with that about the
Father. But we must remember that the purpose
of both the Son and the Spirit is to reveal the
Father to men and not themselves. Yet there is
no ambiguity in the revelations about the Spirit
nor a depreciation of his importance. The rather
he is magnified and glorified. It is lamentable
that in our day the Holy Spirit should have been
so neglected that the use of his name has become
almost the shibboleth of a certain stamp of Christians. Whose fault is it? Some so-called Christians even deny the reality of the Holy Spirit.

The Holy Spirit is frequently mentioned in the
Old Testament. " The Spirit of the Lord is upon
you," Isaiah cried (Isa. 61 : 1) So
Joel predicted and God said: " I
will pour out my Spirit upon all
flesh " (Joel 2 : 28). "Take not thy Holy Spirit
from me," David prayed in his great penitential
Psalm (51 : 11). The Spirit of God is a phrase
often in the mouth of the prophets. Still the
New Testament time is preeminently the dispensation of the Holy Spirit. The apocryphal wisdom of Solomon makes frequent mention of the
Holy Spirit, but Jesus has told us most about
his work.

Not a
New Doctrine

He is not merely an influence simply because he is spoken of as Spirit. God is Spirit, and that argument would destroy the person-
ality or individuality of the Father. **The** When Jesus calls him another Com- **Personality of** forter he clearly sets forth another **the Holy Spirit** person on a par with himself. When Jesus gave the Great Commission he commanded baptism in the name of the Father, Son, and Holy Spirit. If the Father and Son are persons, so is the Spirit. We are not able to give an adequate definition of person as applied to the Trinity, nor for that matter can we adequately describe person at all. The word means mask, then a part played, then the one who plays a part, the individual. We know that we are ourselves separate beings, en-dowed with individual characteristics and re-sponsibilities, though enjoying all of us a common nature. One of our first lessons is the difference between *meum* and *tuum*. Some persons never learn it. In the will we place the seat of conscious power, but clear analysis eludes the psychologist who searches for the spirit of man or of God. The work of the Holy Spirit is likewise conclusive proof that he is personal, and not merely an influ-ence. The Holy Spirit bears witness with our spirits and dwells in us. The Trinity is thus clearly taught, one God and three persons.

The Holy Spirit is the Spirit of God who is himself spirit. It was the Spirit of God who descended on Jesus at his baptism. **Relation to the Father** The Father will send the Holy Spirit when Jesus is gone from earth. The Spirit proceeds from the Father. The Son returns to the Father and the Spirit comes from the Father. The Holy Spirit was in the world in some measure before the ascension of Christ, but it was at Pentecost, the great Pentecost, that the Holy Spirit came in fulness and power. John had said that Jesus would baptize with the Spirit, but the promise was not fully realized till Jesus went up on high. The Spirit was not incarnate as Christ and the "bodily form," like a dove, at the baptism was temporary and symbolic, but he dwells in the Christian, in individuals, and in churches. God gives not the Spirit by measure, but in richness and power. As Jesus revealed the Father while on earth, so the Spirit continues that glorious work and with a great advantage. Jesus, having human form, was here and not there, but the Spirit having no bodily form is omnipresent, *i. e.*, he can dwell in every Christian at the same time. Moreover, Jesus could not stay on earth always. But the Holy Spirit will be with us forever. The term Holy used so often before Spirit has its fullest contrast.

He is absolutely holy and so differs from our spirit, as Jesus said, "Holy Father." He is not only the Spirit of God, but is God. Spirit is more nearly the idea than Ghost, which in modern English brings up the picture of death. He is the Spirit of life, and not the ghost of death. Not only does the Father give the Holy Spirit to them that ask him, but he is more ready to do so than an earthly father is to give good gifts to those who ask him. Do we ask the Father for this high and holy gift? The new yearning for the Holy Spirit in our time is cause for gratitude.

The mystery of the incarnation of Christ is revealed as wrought by the Holy Spirit. On this point Jesus, of course, says nothing. But both Matthew and Luke testify to the brooding investiture of the Holy Spirit, by whose power the Word was made flesh and so he was born of woman. The union of the divine and the human natures in Christ is the great mystery of his person. We know that this essential fact in the Redeemer's incarnation is due to the Holy Spirit, but we must leave it in mystery.

Jesus in his human life was under the guidance of the Holy Spirit in a special way. The descent of the Holy Spirit at the baptism was not the beginning of this influence upon him, but was rather the formal entrance upon the Messianic mission. John was to know the Messiah by this descent. Jesus was led of the Spirit into the wilderness to be tempted of the devil. He went into Galilee full of the Holy Spirit. He wrought his miracles by the Spirit of God. Blasphemy against the Spirit of God was worse than against Jesus, who was also man. Indeed, the ministry of Christ was set over against that of John the Baptist by the Baptist himself as being one characterized by the baptism of the Holy Spirit. John the Baptist was full of the Holy Spirit, and yet he said that the ministry of Jesus should be so much that of the Spirit that his would sink back into obscurity by contrast. As his was marked by water baptism, Christ's would be distinguished by Spirit baptism. Jesus would baptize some with the Spirit and others with fire; the axe lay at the root of the trees; and so the good will stand while the unfruitful will be hewn down and cast into the fire; the wheat will be gathered into the garner, the chaff will be burned with fire unquenchable. Separation then will mark the ministry of Jesus. There will be a twofold baptism, that of the Spirit and that of fire. Jesus himself rejoiced in the Holy Spirit when the Seventy returned from their experimental ministry.

There is an implied inferiority in office on the

part of the Holy Spirit, both to the Father and the Son. In person and nature the Spirit is on a par with the Father, but the Father sends the Holy Spirit and so does Jesus. He spoke of the Spirit "whom I will send from the Father" (John 15 : 26). Once in the upper room after the resurrection he breathed on them and said : " Receive ye the Holy Spirit." This was an earnest of what was to come. The Spirit is to be sent again in the name of Jesus. He is to be another Comforter, just as Jesus had been. Henceforth the new Comforter will take the place of Jesus with believers. Moreover, it is best for them that Jesus go to the Father. Else the Spirit could not come in the new and large sense. And this coming is for the good of all. He will be a true Comforter, Helper, Paraclete, Advocate. It is a hard word to translate, for it combines the idea of advocate and consoler. He will teach us how to plead our cause with God, and will himself plead God's cause with us. The Greek advocate did both of these things with his client. He pleaded the case and taught the client to plead his own cause. We have two Advocates. Christ on high pleads our cause with the Father, and the Spirit on earth pleads the Father's cause with us. God has made every possible provision for the salvation of the sinner and the growth of the Christian.

The Holy Spirit is the teacher about Jesus as Jesus was the teacher of God. Thus we learn the Father in the Son by the Spirit.

Our Apprehension of Christ is by the Spirit Jesus bids us come to him and learn of God ; so the Spirit offers to teach us the riches of Christ. Jesus is the picture of the Father, but the Spirit explains the picture. "If I go, I will send him unto you"(John 16 : 7). Yes, he continues, and when he is come, "he shall glorify me : for he shall take of mine and shall declare it unto you" (John 16 : 14). "He shall bear witness of me" (John 15 : 26). This is the great office of the Spirit. *He can help men to see Christ.* No man has ever seen Christ who has not seen him as the Spirit is able to reveal him.

Pictures of Christ by great artists all fail to catch the real Christ. We hear much about the historical Christ in our day, and historical criticism has done much for the apprehension of Jesus. The figure of Christ now fills the world as it never did before. We can get back behind Calvin and Augustine, and see Jesus as his followers and contemporaries saw him. But even then we have not seen Jesus as he was and is. For his contemporaries crucified him, one of his followers betrayed him, another denied him, and all expected him to set up a temporal Messianic kingdom in Jerusalem. If we had lived then would we have understood Christ? Now, as then, mere historical information, however great, cannot tell all that is to be known about Jesus nor the best that there is to know. Many a man has essayed to write a life of Jesus who has never sat at the feet of Jesus, and who has not chosen the good portion of spiritual fellowship. The spiritual apprehension of Christ as of the truth in Jesus, is the only adequate knowledge of the Saviour. This is to know Jesus and the power of his resurrection. This knowledge of Jesus the Holy Spirit alone can give. As no one can fully reveal the Father save the Son, so no one can fully reveal Jesus save the Holy Spirit. If we would see Jesus now, we need not merely the words of Jesus, but the Spirit of Jesus and the Spirit-blessed messenger.

The Holy Spirit will use men, not angels, to tell the story of Jesus. He impresses the heart directly, even the heart of the unregenerate, but none the less and all the more the gospel preacher is **The Apostolic Teaching** needed and used, a man who has a personal experience of Christ's love to tell. The Spirit is promised to all Christians in the apprehension of Christ and insight into the truth of God. He is the Spirit of truth, and so is concerned with all aspects of truth. Besides the illumination to all Christians in whom he abides, the Spirit is promised in special manner to the apostles and early followers of Jesus. He shall "bring to your remembrance all that I said unto you" (John 14 : 26). How much they had forgotten! "He shall guide you into all the truth" (John 16 : 13), for Jesus had not told them all they needed to know (John 16 : 12). It was a progressive unfolding of the truth about God. The kingdom kept coming more and more. But the Spirit would "teach you all things" (John 14 : 26). They will be qualified to teach Jesus by a larger and richer knowledge of him. It is fifty days in time from the crucifixion to the day of Pentecost, but it is fifty years in psychological and spiritual history. Peter, who had gone into hiding after his disgraceful denial of Christ, becomes the outspoken champion and exponent of Christianity. From a cowardly blasphemer he has turned into a lion of courage. Then he quailed before the rulers; now they quail before him. This revolution in Simon Peter calls for an explanation. The facts alone can give it. Jesus rose from the dead; Peter saw him; the Holy Spirit has flooded his heart. This is revelation. This is inspiration. Here is the first interpretation of Jesus under the guidance of the Holy Spirit. It is like that of Jesus himself, only it is fuller, for the great facts of his atoning death, resurrection, and ascension could not be fully interpreted before they came to pass. First faith had displaced doubt. Then hope had come. Now there is knowledge and power.

It was not till Pentecost that even Peter apprehended Jesus. Before he died Jesus promised that the Holy Spirit would come to bless and guide, to be his successor. After his resurrection and just before his ascension he repeated that promise. He could do so with new emphasis and with special appropriateness. This coming of the Holy Spirit was to be an age-long dispensation. The baptism of the Holy Spirit was to mark the entrance upon the new epoch of expansion in knowledge and growth. The signs accompanying it authenticated the advent of the Spirit. In this sense the baptism of the Holy Spirit as marking a new dispensation is not to be repeated now. It is like the incarnation of Christ. But it is a real baptism of the Spirit every time we actually put ourselves at the service of God's Spirit. It is a missionary promise that needs to be linked to the Great Commission. Jesus charged the disciples to go into all the world and take it for him. Now he renews that command. Then he had said that he would be with them all the days. Now he says that the Holy Spirit will clothe them with power. With this new power

they can and must go unto all the nations, beginning from Jerusalem. Thus Judea, Samaria, and
the uttermost part of the earth will be reached.
This is the horizon that Jesus lifts before his now
rejoicing disciples as he leaves them. Soon he
led them out and ascended on high. The sublime
optimism of Jesus in the face of death and de-
parture from earth is due to his knowledge that
the Holy Spirit will succeed him and carry on the
Christian enterprise. He dared challenge the
kingdom of the world to final struggle, for he knew
his power. He had already overcome the world
and so must the disciples.

The Holy Spirit, then, is to take up the struggle
against the kingdom of Satan. Jesus challenged
Satan and overcame the world. The
**The Spirit
and the World** Holy Spirit is to convict the world
(John 16 : 8 f.). He is to press
Christ on the hearts of men. Sin, righteousness,
and judgment are the things about which the Spirit
will convict men, but sin first and foremost. One
of the deadening effects of sin is that men lose
consciousness about it. After sin comes righteousness as the opposite and the necessary substi-
tute for it. Without righteousness comes judgment for sin. The sense of sin and the need of
righteousness we should press home now, as never
before on the minds of men. The Spirit alone

can reach the hearts of men. Let us use winged words, use all skill and wisdom, and trust the Spirit of God. Vain is our preaching without the convicting power of the Holy Spirit.

After conviction one of two things results, rejection or submission. The Holy Spirit presses on a man his destiny. It is the sublimest of conflicts when the Spirit of God strives with the spirit of man. The two sovereign wills collide. See the struggle in a child's will. No wonder the angels watch and rejoice when man surrenders to God and finds his own best self in God. God respects the human will. Jesus called this experience the new birth. It is a birth by the Spirit of God in the spiritual nature of man. A new heart comes to him and a new life begins. This is the supreme mystery in the Christian life. We cannot explain how the Spirit of God lays hold of the spirit of man, dead in trespasses and sins, and injects new life into him. It is the Spirit that quickens. Herein is the marriage between divine sovereignty and human free agency. We know that God is supreme and that we are responsible. The absolute power of God does not absolve us from our responsibility. We know this and must be content to know no more. Jesus himself found his chief joy in doing the will of the Father. That is the highest virtue.

The Holy Spirit shall dwell in us. With the new birth the Holy Spirit takes up his abode in our souls; our bodies are his temple. Think of that. He carries on the work that he began in us. We are to be sanctified in the realm of the truth, but the work is done by the Holy Spirit. Jesus did not expand this phase of the Spirit's work, as we have it discussed later in Galatians and Romans. But the abiding presence of the Holy Spirit is made clear. The indwelling power of the Spirit is dwelt on also. Jesus even said that the Father and he would make their abode in the hearts of believers (John 14 : 23). Wonder of wonders is this. This blessed indwelling is the work of the Holy Spirit. Thus Jesus will be with his people through all the ages. So also the disciple grows into constant and increasing likeness to his Master. If the Spirit of Christ is in us, we are his now and shall be with him always. The Spirit will make us holy in the end. Sanctification is a process, not a single act. We should seek to be holy. Actually some people think it a bad thing to be holy. This is due to a reaction against a professional holiness which does not command confidence.

We do not need to pray for the coming of the Holy Spirit. The promise of the Father was fulfilled at Pentecost. The Holy Spirit is here and this is his dispensation. We need to put ourselves at the service of the Spirit, so as to be used by him. It is the age of the Holy Spirit. He, not the pope, is the Vicegerent of Christ. He is willing and anxious to bless us and to use us. And he will if we are not full of ourselves, if we are willing to be filled with the power of the living God. We must make room for the Spirit of God. We should live so that the Spirit will love and dwell in us. Jesus will come again. Till he come the Spirit is here to lead men to Christ and thus to the Father. Are we at the service of the Spirit?

He alone is power, for he is God. He uses many conductors for the conveyance of power, and some very weak ones. Can a soul be saved as the result of the preaching of a bad man? What about Judas? We are not responsible for our spiritual ancestors. **The Spirit the Power in Christianity** We do not trust the preacher, but Christ. The wires that run overhead are not the power that moves the cars. The cars do not move themselves. The electricity is the power. We must not mistake machinery for power, nor creed for life. Modern Christianity is highly organized and properly so. The manifold life of to-day calls for varied effort. But there is only one power for all the wheels, for all the engines, for all the weapons in the army of Christ.

It is the Spirit of God. If we look to aught else the wheels will run off, the engines will be power-less. To change the figure we shall use blank cartridges. We shall then have pop-gun sermons instead of torpedoes. On what do we depend for success? No real progress is possible in Christian work that does not help on the kingdom of God. Vain our statistics, our conventions, our schools, our papers, our books, our gifts, our numbers, our gatherings, our emotions unless God be with us, God the Holy Spirit. If we follow his lead and feel the beat of his heart we shall take the world for Christ and do it speedily. Lord Jesus, breathe on us thy Spirit and fill us with the fulness of God. Dwell in us and help us walk with thee.

CHAPTER VII

THE FUTURE LIFE

"I come again, and receive you unto myself, that where I am there ye may be also" (John 14 : 3).

JESUS has more to say about the life that now is than about the life to come, but not because the present life is more important. Far otherwise. With Jesus the chief emphasis is ever on the future state. Present duties are brightened by future hopes. Present woes are darkened by a greater cloud. The satisfaction of the world without God is the pity of it all.

The world is always longing for a voice from the other world to tell the truth about it. Men slip up back-stairs to attics to hear what so-called spiritualists have to say. Yes, and they believe this is scientific, while Christianity is superstition! It is easy to deceive people. They will not believe Moses and the prophets nor the voice from the dead (Luke 16 : 31). Jesus is the real voice from the other world. He came from heaven, where he had been before his incarnation. Repeatedly

Christ speaks of his having come from God, of the glory that he had with the Father before the foundation of the world. He has come by the humble route of human birth, but none the less he existed before his birth. He is the Word of God, the Living Epistle, addressed to men. Will they read him now? Some rejected Christ then and some reject him now, as the Spirit presses him home on men's hearts. He is, therefore, qualified to speak of God and the future life. He may have drawn a veil down between his earthly life and the life in heaven. We do not know how vivid his consciousness was on that point, but we do know that he had this consciousness. More-over, Jesus came back to earth from the grave. He had all that any man could get who has been to the other world, and more. Jesus came back not as mere spirit, but as himself, soul, and body, and as God's own Son, who rightly apprehended the value of this life and the life to be.

Christ is so clear on this point that no expos-itory remarks are necessary. It is worth while, however, to insist on the fact, for
Reality of the Future Life just here is the essence of Christi-anity. If there is no life hereafter, not only is Jesus grievously deceived, but the hopes of men come to naught. All men, save a few materialistic philosophers, have looked for a

life beyond the grave.   If this is only a mirage it
is more than a mockery.   It is true that the hope
of future life is a comforting and ennobling one,
even if untrue.   But the dignity and the serious-
ness of religion vanish if death ends all.   In fact,
Paul said that we are of all men most miserable.
The character, work, and words of Jesus all
guarantee the reality of the future life.   Else he
is either ignorant and a mere deluded man, or a
hypocrite of the worst kind.   The constant assumption in all the words of Jesus is that he was
able to tell the truth about the spiritual life.

There is no Nirvana in the teaching of Christ.
The rather the conscience is described as being
keenly alive in the other world and
memory is all ablaze.   It would be   **The Future**
a comfort to many men if death   **Life is**
Everlasting
could end all.   It is in this delusive
hope that so many commit suicide.   But the
spiritual life is not deadened by death.   The soul
is released from the body and there is a fuller joy
or a keener woe.   There is no hope of an inter-
mediate state.   Lazarus is in Abraham's bosom,
and the rich man is in torment and a great gulf is
fixed between them.   This is the final, not the in-
termediate state.   There is no complete nor partial
cessation of consciousness, but everlasting consciousness in a highly developed state.   Even in

eternal death it is rather eternal dying in the sense
of spiritual agony, not of unconsciousness. Christ
holds out no hope of annihilation of the soul nor
of soul sleeping. Nor does he predicate future
existence only of the redeemed. Both the saved and
the unsaved have immortal spirits, which shall live
on forever.

The man who thinks that this life is the real
life and seeks it, loses his true life. The way to
find true life is to lose one's life
The Real Life in God. Life consists not in the
is Ahead abundance of things that a man
possesses and is more than meat. The soul is the
man's life, and this is worth more than all the
world, not to mention the little part of it that we
can get for a few years. Hence the satisfaction
of present needs, while necessary, should not be at
the expense of, not to say the exclusion of, the
spiritual life. The soul has need of the body but
the body is only the home of the soul. The soul
can live without it and will do so for a while. The
ultimate state of the soul is to dwell in a glorified
body, not this temple of clay. Wonderful as is
the human body it is a prison to the soul. Its
powers are circumscribed and many clogs hinder
the spiritual life. However, the body in itself is
not 'sinful, though sin dwells in the flesh as in the
soul. The essence of sin is in the soul. But the

body will be raised from the tomb, Jesus said. What this body would be he did not say. Paul calls it a spiritual body that had some connection with the natural body. There will be the resurrection both of the just and of the unjust, to life and to death (John 5 : 29). The mystery of the bodily resurrection is after all no greater than the mystery of life itself. The resurrection of Jesus is not specially analogous to our resurrection, though a guarantee of it. But the spiritual man is to rule the bodily man and not to feed itself on "much goods laid up for many years." That is to be a fool. The pity of it is to see so many starved souls around us feeding on the husks that the swine eat. It was this that evoked the pity of Jesus. The swine care not for pearls. But some men find joy in the hidden treasure, the pearl of great price. In some there is a well of water springing up into everlasting life.

Christ conceives of the future state as determined by this life. The time of probation is here, not hereafter. To this end Jesus exhorted men to believe in him. To this end he promises eternal life— indeed, here already we have eternal life. Future probation receives no sanction in the words of Jesus. He expressly denies it when Abraham reminds the wicked rich

The Future Life Conditioned by this Life

man that he had already had his opportunity in
yonder world. It is more just that it is so and
also more merciful. It is true that we are born
with sinful natures and live in a sinful world, and
multitudes have no knowledge of Christ, and are
without God and without hope in the world. But
even the darkest phase of heathenism has more
opportunity than one could reasonably look for in
the future life, even if such opportunity were given.

Here our hearts are undeveloped and in the
formative state ; there is more possibility of being
reached here by a little light than in the future
life in larger and fuller light. Character is slow in
formation but permanent in result. It is character
that fixes destiny. When the character is stamped
in hard lines the powers of resistance to spiritual
light are indefinitely increased. The demons believe and tremble. They know enough to save
even demons if mere knowledge could do that.

No such word fell from the lips of Jesus. He
did say that there would be degrees of punishment, few stripes and many stripes.
Future Punishment is not Corrective The punishment will be tempered
according to the facts of the char-
acter. But our Lord did not share the
sentimental weakness that shrank from the punishment of sin. He knew how holy God is and how
heinous sin is. He used the word "damnation"

and "damnation of hell" (Matt. 23 : 33). He
spoke of everlasting punishment, and used the
same word for "everlasting" that he used when
he spoke of everlasting life (Matt. 25 : 46). We
need not be more merciful in our theology than
Jesus is. He so loved the world that he died for
it. There can be no greater love than this. It is
gratuitous for us to assume that we apprehend
spiritual realities better than Jesus. And yet he
calmly said to the Pharisees that they would die
in their sins unless they believed in him. We
must remember that it cost the blood of God's
Son to make possible the salvation of any. We
must remember also that men are free agents and
have a right to reject life. The destiny goes with
the choice.

The problem of the heathen is serious. But
Jesus has some sheep among them. The infants
who die before the age of responsibility are
surely saved. The heathen who come to age and
die are not condemned because they have not
heard of Jesus, but because they do not live
up to the light which they have. They have nature and they have conscience. The heathen do
not do what they know, nor did the Jew, nor do
we. There is no hope in any of us save in Christ.
But in salvation through Christ the justice of
God is to be maintained and the free will of man

respected. This problem is too high and too deep for us, but at least we are not permitted in the light of it to rail against God because he punishes those who are guilty of sin with a punishment adequate to the sin. God has ordained a moral universe and righteousness is at the base of it. It would be pleasant to cling to what is called "eternal hope," and long for and believe in the ultimate redemption of all men. But there is no Scripture nor moral basis for it. The arguments that overturn eternal punishment overturn eternal life. We must remember that we do not understand how dreadful sin is nor how holy God is. We can trust the God of all the earth to do right.

It is inevitable that judgment meet us if sin is to be punished. The personal condemnation to hell or the welcome to heaven comes at death. There is thus individual **The Judgment** judgment for every one. And yet the Master teaches more than this. He pictures a general judgment day, which would be only confirmatory of what is already true, to be sure, but which would seal publicly and finally the states of all. The sheep will be on the right and the goats on the left (Matt. 25 : 33). So the shepherds of Palestine, crook in hand, now separate their flocks at eventide. The curse will be: "Depart from me," and will be pronounced by the Son of Man who came on earth to save men. He himself will then be the Judge of all the earth. He as King of the kingdom will open and shut the door of hope for good and all. To the sheep he will say, "Come, ye blessed of my Father." The kingdom was prepared for you before the foundation of the world. Now enter it finally and fully. It is the most august of all the scenes in the words of Jesus, this judgment scene in Matt. 25, when all the peoples of the earth shall be gathered before him. There will be many surprises then or at death. But the Judge and King will pronounce the solemn sentence. By their fruits the trees will be judged and the judgment will be final. "And these shall go away into eternal punishment: but the righteous into eternal life" (Matt. 25 : 46).

Does Jesus teach hell? Has the Revised version done away with hell? Now the English word hell originally meant the hidden place, from *helan*, to hide or conceal. The Greek word hades meant precisely this idea. It was the unseen world, not the evil world. To be sure, in the unseen world are both heaven and hell. So the rich man is in hades in torment. So hades was sometimes used of the place of torment as the English word hell is now always. The Revised version has done a service in transliterating hades and confining the term hell to the translation of gehenna. But the revisers have not taken hell out of the teaching of Jesus. It is impossible to take it out. The idea is put in figurative form, it is true, but the figures fall short of the reality, as is true in the case of heaven. Jesus has not said that hell is literal fire, though he calls it the hell of fire and unquenchable fire. He also calls it the place of outer darkness, the place where the worm dieth not. But the fact of hell is not dependent on the literalness of these awful figures, for eternal punishment is hell. The eternal wrath of God is hell. The lashing of the conscience is hell. Jesus means that hell is the abode of lost spirits. But the fact of hell is not conditioned by its being a place, though this is possibly true. Every man makes his own hell and makes it here. Hell begins on earth and is continued hereafter. We need new emphasis on the fact of hell, but let it be scriptural emphasis, not mere theological emphasis. We must always distinguish between a fact and our theory of the fact.

"Because I live, ye shall live also" (John 14 : 19). He is life and is able to give life, for he has life in himself (John 5 : 26). This is our ground of hope. The spiritual appropriation of Jesus is the assimilation of spiritual life. This is to "eat" his flesh and to drink his blood, indeed to "eat" him

The Ground of Eternal Life

(John 6 : 57). Here, then, the Christian is on high and sure, if mystical, ground. The branches are united to the vine. No one can snatch the elect out of the hand of the Redeemer. This is the true " eternal hope " and the only one. This is the way to have life in ourselves. Jesus has life in himself and can give us eternal life. The words of Jesus are spirit and life only because he is spirit and life. Jesus offers himself in the last analysis as the ground of eternal hope. Life comes from life, eternal life from eternal life.

Jesus gives us not many pictures of heaven, though he often alludes to heaven, as when he says "our Father in heaven," "the angels of God in heaven," "joy in heaven," Christ's Picture of Heaven "treasures in heaven." The phrase "kingdom of heaven" is very common in Matthew and is equal in effect to the kingdom of God. God is in heaven and heaven is where God is in his fulness and power. Jesus himself comes from heaven and is going back to heaven. He likewise uses Abraham's bosom as a term for future happiness. So also paradise is a term for heaven. The word heaven is used in two senses, the regions above us and then the abode of the redeemed.

But it is in John fourteen that our Lord has most to say on the subject of heaven. Here he calls it his Father's house. It is a figure surely, but a beautiful one.   Our Father has a great home with many mansions, and there is room for all the children.   The eldest Son has gone back home and he will make ready a place for all the absent loved ones.   As they come home he will welcome them and assures them beforehand that a room will be ready.   He wishes them all to be with him forever in the Father's house.   There is going to be a family reunion on high.   All the absent ones will come back.   The vacant chairs will be occupied.   The vacant seats at the table will be no longer empty.   Moreover, Jesus will come himself and show us the way to the home on high.   He will take us by the hand at the gate of death and lead us over the river and up the hill and into our new home.   That will be heaven, to be with Jesus forever, to see him as he is.   He will then show us the Father in a new way.   We shall be ready to endure the majesty and glory of the surroundings.   All sin will be purged from our hearts.   We shall be pure, and only the pure will be there.   He will introduce us to the saints of old, to Abraham, to Moses, to Elijah, to David, to Isaiah, to John the Baptist, to John the beloved disciple, to Simon Peter, to Paul, to Augustine, to Chrysostom, to Calvin, to Knox, to Spurgeon, to Boyce, to Broadus.   Then the kingdom will have come indeed.   But if this is to be true the kingdom must begin with us here on earth. Heaven must first enter us if we are to enter it. Jesus said that, if he went, he would come again and take us to be with him. "Amen : come, Lord Jesus."

These seven "words" of Jesus are not all that he spoke to men. They are, however, most important for the comprehension of the theology of our Lord. If we rightly understand the great Teacher's message concerning the Father, the Son, Sin, the Kingdom of God, Righteousness, the Holy Spirit, the Future Life, we shall be able easily to construct an orderly and a correct outline of the remaining doctrines. The logic of the life and teachings of Jesus is summed up in his own memorable words : "All things have been delivered unto me of my Father : .. and no one knoweth the Son, save the Father ; neither doth any know the Father, save the Son, and he to whomsoever the Son willeth to reveal him. Come unto me, all ye that labor and are heavy laden, and I will give you rest. Take my yoke upon you, and learn of me ; for I am meek and lowly in heart : and ye shall find rest unto your souls. For my yoke is easy, and my burden is light" (Matt. 11 : 27–30).

INDEX OF SCRIPTURE
REFERENCES

TOPICAL INDEX

BIBLIOGRAPHY

Adamson, Studies in the Mind of Christ, 1898.

James Robertson, The Teaching of Our Lord, 1900.

Horton, The Teaching of Jesus, 1895.

G. B. Stevens, The Teaching of Jesus, 1901.

Wendt, The Teaching of Jesus, 1892.

Jackson, The Teaching of Jesus, 1903.

Moorhouse, The Teaching of Christ, 1891.

Swete, Studies in the Teaching of Our Lord, 1903.

King, The Theology of Christ, 1903.

Seeburg, *Das Evangelien Christi*, 1905.

Stubbs, *Verba Christi*, 1903.

Sanday, The Teaching of Jesus, in article Jesus Christ, in Hasting's Dictionary of the Bible, and in Outlines of the Life of Christ, 1905.

Lancaster, The Creed of Christ, 1905.

Anonymous, The Creed of Christ, 1905.

Tigert, The Christianity of Christ and His Apostles, 1905.

Bosworth, Studies in the Teaching of Jesus and His Apostles, 1900.

Speer, the Principles of Jesus, 1902.

Stier, The Words of Jesus, 1869.

D. Meyer, *Le Christianisme du Christ*, 1883.

A. T. Robertson, The Teaching of Jesus Concerning God the Father, 1904.

Crane, The Teaching of Jesus Concerning the Holy Spirit, 1905.

Ross, The Self-Portraiture of Jesus, 1904.

Bernard, The Central Teaching of Christ, 1897.

Stalker, The Christology of Jesus, 1899.

Foster, The Teaching of Jesus Concerning His Own Mission, 1903.

D'Arcy, Ruling Ideas of our Lord, 1901.

Fairbairn, The Place o' Christ in Modern Theology, 1893.

Gilbert, The Revelation of Jesus, 1899.

Ian Maclaren, The Mind of the Master, 1896.

J. Weiss, *Die Predigt Jesu von Reiche*, 1892.

Krop, *La Pensée de Jésus sur le Royaume de Dieu*.

Titius, *Jesu Lehre vom Reiche Gottes* 1895.

Schnedermann, *Jesu Verkundigung und Lehre vom Reiche Gottes in ihrer geschichtlichen Bedeutung dargestellt. Bde I., II.,* 1895.

Vos, The Teaching of Jesus Concerning the Kingdom and the Church, 1903.

Mathews, The Social Teaching of Jesus, 1897.

Heuver, The Teaching of Jesus Concerning Wealth, 1903.

Peabody, Jesus and the Social Question, 1901.

Haupt, *Die Eschatologischen Aussagen Jesu in den Synoptischen Evangelien*, 1895.

Muirhead, The Eschatology of Jesus, 1904.

Briggs, The Ethical Teaching of Jesus 1904.

Hermann, *Die Sittlichen Weisungen Jesu*, 1904.

Grimm, *Die Ethik Jesu*, 1903.

Peabody, Jesus Christ and Christian Character, 1905.

Bachmann, *Die Sittenlehre Jesu*, 1904.

Fluegel, *Die Sittenlehre Jesu*, 1888.

Broadus, The Ethical Teaching of Jesus, Lecture II., in Jesus of Nazareth, 1889.

Zenos, The Teaching of Jesus Concerning Christian Conduct, 1905.

Hyde, Jesus' Way, 1902.

Ehrhardt, *Die Grundcharakter der Ethik Jesu*, 1895.

Schuerer, *Die Predigt Jesu Christi in ihren verhältniss zum A. T. und zum Judenthum*, 1882.

Bousset, *Jesu' Predigt in ihrer Gegensatz zum Judenthum*, 1892.

Burrell, The Teaching of Jesus Concerning the Scriptures, 1904.

Saphir, Christ and the Scriptures.

MacFarland, Jesus and the Prophets, 1905.

Rae, How Jesus Handled Holy Writ, 1902.

Mead, Christ and Criticism.

Nicoll, The Church's One Foundation, 1905.

Ellicott, *Christus Comprobator*.

Bischoff, *Jesus und die Rabbinen*, 1905.

Vaughan, Characteristics of Christ's Teaching, 1866.

Special books on the Sermon on the Mount by Augustine (Trench), Boyd-Carpenter, Genung, Mackintosh, Tholuck, Achelis, Steinmeyer, Heinrici, Bacon, Schenck, Griffith-Jones, Grauvert, Shorthouse, Votaw (Hastings' Dictionary), Lyttleton, Ibbeken, H. Weiss, Bossuet, Gore, Kaiser, Monneron, Harnisch, Grüllich.

The Parables also have received frequent treatment, as in the works of Drummond, Calderwood, Bruce, Goebel, Lisco, Trench, W. M. Taylor, Arnot, Bourdillon, Thompson, Dods, Salmond, Resker, Tait, Juelicher, Steinmeyer, Habershon, Bugge, Weinel, Lang, Buisson, Guthrie, Beyschlag, Thiersch, Tamm, Freystedt, Fiebig, Plummer (Hastings' Dictionary).

On the death of Christ see:

Schwartzkopff, The Prophecies of Jesus Christ Relating to His Death, etc., 1897.

Babut, *La Pensée sur la Mort*, 1897.

Denney, The Death of Christ, 1902.

Hoffmann, *Das Selbstbewusstsein Jesu*, 1904.

Schuerer, *Das Messianische Selbstbewusstsein Jesu*.

Baldensperger, *Das Selbstbewusstsein Jesu*, 1892.

See also the various books on Biblical Theology of the New Testament.